TEACHING AND STRESS

TEACHING AND STRESS

EDITED BY
Martin Cole and
Stephen Walker

OPEN UNIVERSITY PRESS
Milton Keynes · Philadelphia

Open University Press
Celtic Court
22 Ballmoor
Buckingham MK18 1XW

and
1900 Frost Road, Suite 101
Bristol, PA 19007, USA

First Published 1989
Reprinted 1990

Copyright © The Editors and Contributors 1989

British Library Cataloguing in Publication Data

Cole, Martin
    Teaching and stress.
    1. Great Britain. Schools. Teachers. Stress
    I. Title II. Walker, Stephen, 1944–
    371.1'04

    ISBN 0-335-09548-8
    ISBN 0-335-09547-X pbk

Library of Congress Cataloging-in-Publication Data

Teaching and stress / edited by Martin Cole and Stephen Walker.
        p.   cm.
    Includes index.
    ISBN 0-335-09548-8.   ISBN 0-335-09547-X (pbk)
    1. Teachers – Great Britain – Job Stress – Congresses.   2. Teacher
moral – Great Britain – Congresses.   I. Cole, Martin, 1944–
II. Walker. Stephen, 1944–
LB2840.2.T43   1989
371.1'001'9–dc19   88-23675
                                                                   CIP

Typeset by Rowland Phototypesetting Limited
Bury St Edmunds, Suffolk
Printed in Great Britain by
The Alden Press Limited, Oxford

CONTENTS

CONTRIBUTORS

Neil Boot	Maxwell and Cox Associates, Sutton Coldfield, West Midlands
Susan Capel	Department of Education, Bedford College of Higher Education
Binoy Chakravorty	Senior Medical Officer, Community Health, of a UK District Health Authority
Martin Cole	CRIT, Newman and Westhill Colleges, Birmingham
Sue Cox	Centre for Extension Studies, Loughborough University
Tom Cox	Director, Stress Research Group, University of Nottingham
Jack Dunham	Department of Further Professional Studies, University of Bristol
José Esteve	Director, Institute of Educational Sciences, University of Málaga, Spain
Andrea Freeman	Edge Hill College of Higher Education, Ormskirk
Eric Hall	School of Education, University of Nottingham
Chris Kyriacou	Department of Education, University of York
Stephen Walker	CRIT, Newman and Westhill Colleges, Birmingham
David Woodhouse	Centre for Social and Moral Education, University of Leicester
Peter Woods	Professor of Education, Open University
Arthur Wooster	School of Education, University of Nottingham

ACKNOWLEDGEMENTS

The Centre for Research in Teaching is based at Newman and Westhill Colleges, Birmingham. We are grateful for the support of colleagues in the colleges and of the two Principals. We are also indebted to Sarah Wattison and Janet Cowsill for their cheerful willingness to meet imposs- ible demands in the preparation of the manuscript of this book. Finally, thanks are due to two highly successful stress managers, Lynda Cole and Sandra Walker.

A version of some parts of Training Teachers to Tackle Stress by José Esteve in Chapter 8 first appeared in the *European Journal of Teacher Education* (1986), **9** (3).

INTRODUCTION: STUDYING STRESS

Martin Cole and Stephen Walker

At the time of writing, it hardly seems necessary for us to devote these introductory sentences to a justification for a book about teachers and stress. The topic is apparently front-page news! Or so it would seem from recent features on BBC Radio 2's Jimmy Young Show and on an edition of a Radio 4 phone-in programme devoted to education.

Perhaps the two-day conference on 'Teachers and Stress' (held in September 1987) on which this book is based, played some part in bringing the topic to the attention of the news media. The origins of the conference lay, however, principally in a desire to promote forms of 'action research' in which those with a concern with stress in teaching worked together to further understanding and develop positive practical policy. This intention represented one of the first ventures of the Centre for Research in Teaching (CRIT), which was founded by members of the Newman and Westhill association of colleges in Birmingham in 1986. The Centre's aim is to promote collaborative programmes of action research focusing on the day-to-day problems identified by teachers themselves.

It was no surprise to ourselves that the first topic put forward by teachers for consideration by CRIT was stress in teaching. Although both of us had experienced stress as teachers in urban comprehensive schools in the 1960s and 1970s, it did not become a central issue in our thinking about teachers and teaching until the 1980s. One of us (Martin Cole) had spent a year at the beginning of the decade researching teachers' thinking about their work through a programme of unstructured confidential interviews conducted in teachers' homes. This research had not been conceived with stress in mind, but the overwhelming impression received from these randomly selected teachers was of widespread and powerful feelings of bitterness, frustration, disillusionment and low morale. Given a sympathetic and confidential ear, teachers would spend several hours of the evening, and sometimes the night, seizing the opportunity to give vent to feelings that starkly exposed the considerable levels of stress their occupation entailed.

Another formative experience during the growth of our concern with stress was working with a group of teachers during a one-term module of an in-service B.Ed. course which, while nominally concerned with classroom interaction, was rapidly turned by the students into an analysis of stress in teaching. During this course we rather nervously suggested that students might read a brief article that David Hargreaves had written in *New Society* as long ago as 1978 under the title 'What Teaching Does to Teachers'. Our timidity arose from the fact that the article portrayed teachers in a way that we thought very depressing, though accurate and sympathetic. It spoke of the way teachers 'talk in a highly didactic manner' and become 'petty' and 'bad learners'. There was a 'progressive exhaustion' which 'breeds an out-of-school apathy'. 'A cycle of debilitation and demoralisation' helped to see that 'the way is paved for the worn-out teacher to become just plain dull' so that 'socially teachers become a drag'. Many teachers, Hargreaves thought, responded to the stresses of their work by 'personal withdrawal'; they 'become alienated from their job and withdraw into defensive strategies . . . coping within a very circumscribed set of objectives'; 'innovations' were 'instinctively treated as suspect' in a 'conservative policy of survival'.

It came as something of a surprise when, on reading this gloomy portrait, our teacher-students reacted with excited approval. 'Yes, that's the way it is', they almost all agreed. Hargreaves' article had, they felt, captured perfectly the essence of being a teacher. Copies of the article were requested for showing to colleagues at school and the following week we were told how whole staffrooms had passed the article around and repeated the acclamation.

If the stresses of teaching in the 1970s had been taking the drastic toll Hargreaves had described in 1978, teaching in the 1980s seems certain to have exacted a still greater price. Had all other things been equal (which they probably were not), the rapid rate of policy change, the relative decline in salaries, status and promotion prospects and the insecurity of the redeployment threat posed by falling rolls would alone have been likely to exacerbate teacher stress. Perhaps the industrial action by teachers in the mid-1980s should be seen partly as an index of the degree of stress felt by teachers. We must recognize, though, that this action was at the same time a considerable *source* of stress among teachers, challenging individuals' identities as vocational professionals and creating tensions within staffrooms.

And so we have arrived at a situation in the latter half of the 1980s where stress has become a major talking point in the profession. It has been the subject of major debates in the national conferences of the main teaching unions in 1988 and, as we noted earlier, has now attracted the full glare of mass media attention. There appears, too, to be an insatiable demand among teachers for courses that address the problem of stress.

Of course, a cynic might argue that stress in teaching is an invention of union propagandists anxious to lend weight to their pay claims; even some within the profession see the topic as a 'flavour of the month' which will be abandoned in favour of something else in a year or two's time. Later in this volume, however, it will be argued both that teaching will always be inherently stressful and that the radical changes in the education system currently occurring are likely, on balance, to increase rather than reduce levels of stress.

It may well be true, though, that as far as the mass media are concerned, the present emphasis on stress will prove to be a passing fad. The last few years have seen a burgeoning of newspaper reports, magazine articles, Sunday supplement features and TV programmes about stress in general – in both domestic and a range of occupational settings. Perhaps this topic, like 'lead in the air', 'saving whales' and polyunsaturates, will also fade into the background to be revivified only occasionally when news of more jazzy issues is thin. For the moment though, 'stress' has a high profile in the mass media and this may have benefits in terms of drawing attention to the problems of teaching and thus encouraging the allocation of resources to researching and then tackling stress in teaching.

Mass media attention to stress also, however, has a dark side. It simplifies and it sensationalizes. These effects were well illustrated the day before the 'Teachers and Stress' conference opened when one of the television companies telephoned CRIT to request a spokesman who could be interviewed for a breakfast programme next morning. 'And would you be able to find one or two teachers who suffer from stress to accompany you to the studio?' the request continued. Our unwillingness and inability to supply the requisite evidence in the form of stressed teachers may be part of the explanation for an editorial decision made that evening to drop the item. Apart from the obvious objections to the voyeuristic nature of the proposed item, what concerned us was the assumption we feared underlay the request that stress among teachers was simply about the failure to cope of a few individuals. We hoped the conference would help to spread the understanding that *all* teachers experience stress to some degree. Our dealings with the TV company helped to persuade us that this book should not bear the title 'Teachers and Stress', which we had chosen for the conference, but rather 'Teaching and Stress'.

There is a constant danger that media treatment of stress will simplify and sensationalize the matter into one where stress is seen as a pathological state: there is something 'wrong' with the individuals who experience it. Locating the 'problem' of stress in individuals is half way to blaming them for their malaise. We shall be at pains in our editorial comments throughout this book to expose the dangers inherent in a concept like stress, particularly with regard to this propensity for 'blaming the victim'. This is particularly important in relation to teachers' stress, since it has become common practice for politicians and their camp-followers within the mass media to lay the blame for a host of social as well as educational evils at the door of teachers.

We must not allow discussion of stress, too, to be turned into another stick with which to beat teachers. As others will argue in this volume, stress is the product of individuals' interaction with their environment. A failure to address the teaching environment – schools, education systems, whole societies and their political systems – is not only an intellectual flaw, it is politically insidious.

As editors we have seen it as our duty to remind the reader throughout this volume that stress – the way we define it and the assumptions we make about it – is a highly problematic and a highly dangerous concept. With this caveat in mind, the reader should find in the chapters that follow a variety of perspectives on stress that is not only informative but also provocative.

PART 1

UNDERSTANDING STRESS IN TEACHING

1 THE CONDITIONS OF STRESS

Comment: Just because you suffer stress, doesn't mean you're a bad person.

At certain times, certain words take on great power and significance. Certain words seem to catch the mood of the moment: drop-out, laid-back, yuppy, hip. They come and go and are often seized by media manipulators, hyped and then discarded. Stress is one such word. It is difficult to open a newspaper or to switch on the television today without being confronted by some image of a face lined with anxiety, pain, tension or guilty incompetence. Housewives feel stress – and so do the pressed executive, the commuter, the teenager and the teacher. Paradoxically, we are sold stress as both unavoidable and yet undesirable. And what makes the image on sale particularly dangerous – and wrong – is that it tends to represent stress as a personal failure, as an essential inadequacy in the victim, the individual feeling stressed.

If we are to avoid giving support to this view, we need an alternative. We need to develop an understanding of teachers, teaching and stress, in which rather than teachers being labelled as both inadequate and culpable if they admit to stress, instead they are seen as making fairly normal and predictable responses to stressful experiences. This book begins, therefore, with a chapter which tries to explore the question 'What makes teaching stressful?' as opposed to 'What makes teachers stressed?' This is not just playing with words. It is, in fact, based on a critique of popular analysis and images of stress which emphasize the personal and neglect the situational. It attempts to give a more systematic definition of the concept of teacher stress and to ask what makes teaching particularly stressful, both generally and at specific stages of educational development and change.

This attempt at definition is not without danger. The concepts developed in analysis are frequently hijacked by those seeking to lay the blame for the ills of education at the door of inefficient or inadequate teachers. Thus, terms like teacher stress are used as weapons against teachers rather than as concepts which describe the conditions of teaching. Or, 'burnout' can be used to point to the teachers' lack of energy and worth rather than to how life in schools and classrooms consumes personal resources and individual talent. So, a note of caution from the very start. In one sense, teachers are already 'natural' victims. As Esteve observes in this first chapter:

If everything goes well, parents think their children are good pupils, but if things go badly, they think that the teacher is a bad teacher.

But not only bad teachers experience stress, and not only good teachers avoid stress – it depends on the conditions in which teachers work.

TEACHER BURNOUT AND TEACHER STRESS

José Esteve

Imagine a group of rally drivers who have to drive at high speed throughout the race. Then let's suppose that, without prior warning, all the traffic signs are changed and that, in addition, new ones are added which do not appear in the Highway Code and which, to them, are totally unknown. Their first reaction is surprise. Then they begin to react with hostility. Finally, they end up with their nerves shattered because of the accumulation of tension; they feel bewildered by it all, or, at least, seek an explanation for what has happened. If, on top of all this, the organizers know nothing about the signs which have been changed and side with the spectators in criticizing the drivers for their slowness and the numerous mistakes they have made during the race, then, understandably, there is no knowing what their reaction will be. There will be some who consider giving up: the best-placed ones will try to adapt to the new conditions in the continuing hope of winning; others will become aggressive or simply feel helpless or begin to feel that they are the victims of a huge joke directed at them. In any case, the word 'burnout' would sum up the combined reactions of the group with the majority of them feeling totally bewildered.

Imagine a group of actors in period costume performing a classical work. Suppose now that a new backcloth covers the back of the stage. It is fluorescent pink and decorated with huge figures of Donald Duck and his three nephews. Their reaction would be the same as that of the rally drivers: surprise, aggression, tension and bewilderment. What should they do? Carry on reciting lines in rhyme, dragging around their long robes and occasionally point at Donald Duck to say pompously, 'Look yonder, a thousand horsemen approach!'? Should they ask the audience to stop laughing and listen to the lines? The real problem lies in the fact that, independently of who produced the situation, it is the actors who have to face the audience and who have to acquit themselves as best they can, hopefully with a modicum of success. The reactions thus produced will be mixed, as in the case of the rally drivers, but the word 'burnout' will also serve here as a general term, to sum up the feelings of a group of actors faced with a set of circumstances which force them to make fools of themselves in the course of their work.

Just like the drivers and actors I have described, teachers in our society find themselves faced by circumstances which force them to do their job badly. They are also, as with our examples, subject to criticism which, without bothering to take into consideration these same circumstances, places the blame for the shortcomings of the education system fairly and squarely on teachers. The phrase 'teacher burnout' has become a catchphrase in educational literature and includes all the reactions, apathy, aggression, anxiety, neurosis, defeatism or sheer bloody-mindedness, which can be observed in today's teachers, now totally disorientated as a professional body.

An analysis of this phenomenon should not be seen merely as an exercise in complacency on the part of teachers in the face of the problems which beset teaching. There are three clearly defined functions. First, is that of helping teachers to overcome the bewilderment they feel. If, as seems to be the case, the situation has changed and we are obliged to rethink the role we play, then an analysis of that situation and of the difficulties we have to face will surely help us to come up with suitable answers to the new questions posed. Many of the solutions will probably be difficult to put into practice on an individual basis, but even in the case of the teacher in isolation, a more thorough knowledge of the nature of the problem will help to avoid the feeling of disorientation, and will aid the formulation of solutions.

Secondly, the study of 'teacher burnout' serves to call society's attention to the problem: parents, the media, and above all local and national education authorities, can thus be made to understand the new problems facing today's teachers. As we shall see, an important element in the growth of the problem is the lack of support. Society, at the same time, criticizes and washes its hands of the education of its young and tries to make teachers solely responsible, when, in many cases, the problems are of society and require social solutions.

Thirdly, only by studying the causes can we come up with a plan of action which goes beyond mere well-intentioned suggestions, which is coherent and based on scientific analysis and which will ultimately be capable of improving teachers' working conditions. Action is needed, simultaneously, on various fronts – teacher training, in-service training, resources and a reconsideration of the relationship between responsibility, working hours and salaries.

Concern for educational standards is voiced increasingly. At the same time, a recent Organization for Economic Cooperation and Development (OECD) report (1983) makes mention of the low morale among teachers. While the growth of teacher burnout continues, it is unlikely that teaching standards will improve. A demoralized army never won a battle. For this reason, at the present, where there *is* good quality teaching, it is as a result of the goodwill and the determination of teachers, who, instead of giving in to the temptation to abandon the struggle, throw themselves into their work enthusiastically and, by their efforts, make up for the deficiencies in the system.

Continuing development in the sciences and the need to include new content will mean constant updating and teachers will have to accept radical changes in the development of, and the way they think about, their profession. If something is not done about the lack of direction felt by teachers, to keep pace with the coming changes, then the problem of 'teacher burnout' will increase and the quality of teaching will become steadily worse as teachers become more and more demoralized. Good quality teaching, it must not be forgotten, will be increasingly necessary to meet the specialist needs of a changing society.

In a paper published in 1985, the well-known German comparativist, Wolfgang Mitter, refers to the realization of the fact that there is a 'phase of disenchantment', which he believes is a crucial factor in the practice of teaching in education systems in the West and which is beginning to make itself apparent in the Socialist states of Eastern and Central Europe. Mitter attributes this situation to the low value placed on teacher training and observes that, weighing up the present situation from an international, comparativist point of view, one is inclined to a pessimistic, rather than an optimistic conclusion. In 1982 the American, Blase, was already talking about a 'degenerative cycle in teaching efficiency', produced by a combination of various social and psychological factors and which was beginning to become apparent in present-day teaching.

Of course, 'teacher burnout' has been a talking point for years, although admittedly it was not until the beginning of the 1980s that it repeatedly became the focus of attention in the principal international educational publications. Nevertheless, in the last 6 or 7 years, we have seen a growth of concern in this subject which has resulted in more than 500 bibliographic references in the principal sources of information about education. The expression 'teacher burnout' (*malaise enseignant*, *el malester docente*), is one of the most widely used in bibliography nowadays, describing as it does the permanent, negative effects upon teachers' personalities arising from the social and psychological conditions under which teachers exercise their profession.

In this chapter I intend to broach the subject under three different headings:

1 Identification of the nature of 'teacher burnout' and an analysis of

the symptoms or 'indicators' which prove the existence of this 'degenerative cycle' in teaching efficiency.

2 A study of the effects of 'teacher burnout' on the personality of the teacher.

3 An evaluation and description of the guidelines and strategies which have been developed to tackle the problem and reduce the negative effects of 'teacher burnout'.

The symptoms of teacher burnout

Recent investigation into the subject has usually distinguished between two groups of causative factors of 'teacher burnout'. *Primary factors* are those which have a direct effect on the teacher *in the classroom* and which result in tension connected with the feelings and with negative emotions. *Secondary factors* are environmental, i.e. they affect the *situation* in which teaching takes place. The action of this second group of factors is indirect and affects teaching efficiency by diminishing the teacher's motivation, involvement and the amount of effort he/she is willing to put into the job.

However, it is worth pointing out at this stage that recent research has unanimously emphasized the importance of these secondary factors, given that the problems which exist in the classroom are considered to be both 'normal' and the responsibility of the teacher, whereas secondary factors are more disconcerting and give rise to more feelings of helplessness, by virtue of the fact that nothing can be done about them by the individual – they are brought about by forces within society. In isolation they are relatively unimportant, but *en masse* they have a profound effect on the teacher's self-image and the view he/she may have of the profession, bringing about an identity crisis which may eventually lead to self-deprecation.

Because of the fact that they are general in nature and affect the teaching situation rather than the individual, I shall deal with these secondary factors first, moving on later to look at the primary factors, which are more concrete and more directly related to the practice of teaching.

SECONDARY OR ENVIRONMENTAL FACTORS

We could sum up the role played by these environmental factors with respect to teacher burnout by this general idea: accelerated social changes have had a profound effect on the part played by teachers in the teaching process, without many teachers having known how to adapt themselves to these changes. In addition, administrations have come up with no strategies of action for coping with this new situation – above all in the training of teachers, where no effort has been devoted to answering the demands created by the aforementioned changes. The most obvious result of all this is the worry felt by teachers about the meaning and aims of the job they do. Let us look at the most obvious symptoms or 'indicators' of this situation.

1 Changes in the role of the teacher and of the traditional agents of social integration

During the past 15–20 years, a truly historical process has been going on, in which the demands made on teachers to accept new responsibilities have been steadily increasing. At the same time, a parallel process of withdrawal from educational responsibility has also been going on, both in the community in general and, in particular, within the family. This increase in teachers' responsibilities has not been accompanied by the necessary changes in their training, changes which would teach them to cope with these new demands. The means which teachers have at their disposal have similarly remained unchanged and administrations have not made the necessary changes within their structures to adapt to the new circumstances. The result has been, as Goble and Porter (1980) point out, an increase in the confusion about exactly *what* it is that teachers are supposed to be able to do and about the wide-ranging and complex role that society has entrusted to them.

Still along the same lines, Claude Merazzi (Director of a major Swiss teacher-training college) has defended the theory that, in the present circumstances, one of the most important functions of those who teach, as far as society is concerned, is their capacity to take on situations which involve conflict. This seems to suggest that a new requirement in the training of teachers is that they be taught to live in the face of conflict.

Merazzi's (1983) thesis was based on three fundamental facts. The first is the evolution or transformation of the traditional agents of social integration – basically, the family. The enormous increase in the number of working women has had a number of implications:

- a reduction in the amount of time spent with the children;
- a reduction in the size of families; and
- a reduction in the involvement in the task of education on the part of older brothers, uncles, aunts and grandparents.

This situation has led to teachers having to take into consideration substantial voids in the field of primary social integration, areas which have been left neglected.

Secondly, is the change in the role of the teacher as a transmitter of knowledge which basically springs from the appearance of other power-ful sources of information like the television and other mass media. Teachers now find themselves confronted with the necessity of having to integrate the information-giving potential of these new media, thus modifying their traditional role.

Thirdly, is the need to redefine values and objectives within education. In effect, this is characterized at present by the division of popular opinion over which values scholastic institutions ought to encourage and by which they ought to be governed. In today's pluralist society, quite different social groups, supported by powerful means of communication, define very differently the models of the school, education and society, which they consider to be desirable. Teachers, whichever model of education or system of values they may choose, will always find them-selves questioned and doubted from some quarter. The problem becomes all the more acute when teachers have not made a deliberate choice as to the type of education which they wish to produce, exercising their pro-fession without defining clearly what it is that seems to be 'educational', which values they wish to encourage and which, on the other hand, they seek to repress or to fight openly.

At least teachers who have a clear idea of the educational goals which they wish to follow, although they may be challenged, can be consoled by the fact that they know what they want. Usually in these cases, the effort of having to explain and objectivize one's educational theories is enough to provide one with a comprehensive 'armour' with which to defend one's actions from outside criticism.

It is true to say that teachers today are obliged to think objectively about, and define clearly, their educational objectives. In the first place, this is because a 'convergent' form of society, in which the unifying nature of education in such fields as language, culture and behaviour is all-important, has given way to a 'divergent' society which demands so much diversification in the work of the teacher. Have a look at a state school secondary class and you will see punks, rockers, new romantics, Madonna fans and many more. The difference between 'mods' and 'heavy metal freaks' becomes important because behind every one of these 'urban tribes' there exists not only a particular way of dressing, but also a concept of life based on a specific value system. It is not at all easy, especially as these tribes and subcultures flower, flourish and wither with ever-increasing rapidity.

Some teachers hanker after the good old days when only 'nice kids' were seen in classrooms. The fact is, that for the first time in history, schooling is a reality for 100 per cent of the population and the advantages of the uniformity brought about by the restriction of access to upper- and middle-class children have been wiped away. Teachers have to make the effort to criticize their own middle-class mentality if they are to spare themselves a nasty shock when confronted with this new diversity. In other cases, they have to take on tasks which are unknown in the students' own social environment, whatever it may be. It is no lie to say that, confronted with such diversity, it is more and more important to define exactly what it is that one is trying to achieve.

But there is yet more. Ever more frequently, the teacher is confronted in class by the different forms of social behaviour which have come to be known collectively as the multicultural, multilingual society.

To be a teacher in the outskirts of any of the large European cities today is to teach a mixture of pupils, united only by immigration, who have received their modes of social interaction in different cultures and possibly in different languages. Should the Catalonian teacher uproot from their original culture the Andalusian children in his class? Should the Parisian teacher give up the class on the pork industry, in deference to the five Moroccans, four Algerians, two Tunisians and the single Turk in the class? The teacher in the multiracial, multicultural society must solve problems whose solutions will always run the risk of being challenged. Those who question the diversity in society pose new problems for the teacher. As Merazzi pointed out, it is important to equip them to face and deal with conflict. Meanwhile, as the 1981 International Labour Organization (ILO) report pointed out, it is unjust to reproach them for being unable to meet the challenges set by a world in rapid transformation, especially when they do not have at their disposal the means to be able to meet them adequately.

2   Increasing contradictions in the role of the teacher

The above-mentioned changes mean a profound and demanding challenge for the teacher, who is obliged to think in new terms in order to live up to these new expectations. This situation is aggravated by the fact that teachers are often faced with the situation of having to combine various roles, roles which are contradictory and which demand that they maintain an extremely precarious balance between various positions. Thus, we find that society demands that teachers play variously the role of friend, colleague, companion and helper in general in the development of the student, a position which is incompatible with the role of selector and evaluator which has also been entrusted to them. The development of the individuality of each student may well be incompatible with the demands of social integration, when these imply a predomination of the rules of the group, or when the scholastic institution functions in accordance with demands made on it by society, or by the political or economic forces of the moment. Another frequent contradiction that helps to further the discomfort felt by many teachers is when they work within an institution where they are in disagreement on personal grounds with the form in which it functions or with the values therein encouraged, especially since, when meeting parents and students, the teacher is considered to be a representative of that institution.

We are dealing here with long-standing contradictions which may perhaps be considered to be part and parcel of the business of teaching; but accelerated social changes have, at the present moment, brought about an accumulation of the contradictions which exist in the system of education. As Faure (1973) points out, for the first time in history, society is not asking those who educate to prepare the new generations for conditions which exist at present, but for the needs of a future society which, as yet, does not exist.

When our surroundings are stable, we can, or at least most of us can, cope with them. However, when they begin to change rapidly, even the most healthy among us will find it difficult to avoid the ensuing stress. Toffler (1970) has already warned us about the tension and disorientation produced in people when they are obliged to make rapid changes in too short a time. His description of the disconcerting effect upon the individual when he is moved out of a cultural framework which is familiar to him and in which he has, up to that time, existed and then placed in an environment completely different from his own, without any hope of returning to the previous surroundings he so longs for, could easily be applied to the situation in which hundreds of teachers now find themselves. It is not only a matter of older teachers looking back wistfully to the good old days of certainty in the school of the 'convergent' society. There are also many young teachers who see their companions who studied Latin or Greek in a position a long way removed from the pre-eminent one which they enjoyed a few years ago; and there are others who are asking, to put it simply, if they are not wandering without students, as were the teachers of French who, only a few years ago, monopolized the demand for modern languages. Who will be next, philosophy teachers?

3 Change in the attitude of society towards the teacher

Patrice Ranjard (1984) sums up the content of his interesting article, 'Les enseignants persécutés', by stating that teachers, as far as their work is concerned, feel themselves to be under attack and live, collectively, dominated by feelings of persecution. And this feeling, according to Ranjard, is not without objective reasons, given that 'teachers are persecuted by the development of a society which forces profound changes upon their profession'. But it is not only the role of the teacher that has changed – within the social context in which they exercise their profession the expectations, support and judgement of this social context of teachers have also been changed.

Martin Cole (1985) speaks of the judgement of teachers by society in a paper which bears the significant title of 'A crisis of identity: Teachers in times of political and economical change'. As an example, he recounts the explicit allusions made by British politicians, on British TV, that teachers and the education system were to blame for the vandalism of British fans in the Heysel stadium in Brussels. Along the same lines, in the 1981 ILO report, 'Work and Conditions in the Teaching Profession', the weakening of society's support for teachers is made clear. The same report considers it unjust to blame teachers for not being up to the challenges offered by a rapidly changing world, particularly if they do not have at their disposal the means they need to deal with them.

However, society's judgement of teachers has become generalized. From the politicians responsible for education to the mass media and even the pupils' parents, everyone seems quite happy to think of the teacher as being the one responsible for the many deficiencies and general unease of an education system whose first victims are in fact teachers themselves.

The days have long since passed when parents accompanied their children in the first few days at school and, in the presence of the child, made manifest their unconditional support for the teacher in the process of education which had just begun. At the moment, an accident which occurs during a school outing, the making public of the graffiti written by their children on the back of the toilet door or the recommendation of reading matter considered by the parents to be suspicious, could land the teacher in court.

It is quite true to say that the evaluations made of what the teacher has accomplished are only ever negative. If teachers do a good job, giving over more hours of their time than the normal working day, rarely is this extra effort appreciated; however, when, on the other hand, teaching 'fails', often because of a series of circumstances under which the teacher cannot succeed, the failure is immediately personalized, making the teacher responsible for all the circumstances. If everything goes well, parents think that their children are good pupils, but if things go badly, they think that the teacher is a bad teacher.

In the same way, the opinion that society has of the teacher has undergone a change. Not too long ago teachers, and especially teachers who had a University degree, were thought very highly of, both as educated people and as members of society. Their knowledge, self-sacrifice and vocation were esteemed. But now, our society tends to base social status on income, and the ideas of knowledge, self-sacrifice and vocation have lost their value as far as society is concerned. For many parents the fact that someone has chosen to be a teacher is not indicative of a vocation but merely an 'alibi' for their having been unable to do 'anything better'; that is to say, to do something else which would make more money. Certainly, their salaries constitute yet another element in the identity crisis which faces teachers. In all Western European countries, those who teach receive remuneration markedly inferior to other professionals with similar qualifications.

4 Uncertainty about the objectives of the education system and the furthering of knowledge

The evolution of the social framework has meant a change in the *raison d'être* of scholastic institutions, and the consequent adaptation to that change on the part of pupils, teachers and parents. As Ranjard (1984) pointed out, 'it is absurd to maintain within mass education the objectives of a system designed for the education of an elite'.

Indeed, a few years ago, the holding of a University degree or of secondary education qualifications assured students of a certain social status, with the corresponding remuneration. One of the effects of present-day mass education is the impossibility of guaranteeing all students a job commensurate with their qualifications. If, then, selection does not depend on qualifications and the level of education, isn't it something of a contradiction to carry on with a selective system of education, based on competition?

The change also affects the level of motivation the teacher can expect and utilize in his students. Fifteen years ago a University lecturer could encourage his students by assuring them that their future place in society would depend upon their work as students. Nowadays, unemployment would make a nonsense of this type of reasoning. Many of those who teach have coped with this uncertainty by pointing out that circumstances have indeed changed, thus making redundant their desire to work towards objectives which no longer correspond to the circumstances existing in society today.

Finally, among the elements which contribute to teacher burnout, in so far as they affect the role of the teacher, I should like to turn to the problem of the continuing advance of knowledge.

It is not only a matter of bringing up-to-date that which is taught in order to avoid repeating material which is of such a superficial nature that the teacher is exposed to ridicule, it goes much further than that – in-depth knowledge of any subject is made extraordinarily difficult, to the point where it affects the teacher's self-confidence. Who can be sure of teaching, at any given moment, the latest discoveries to be made in that field of knowledge? Or even worse, who can be sure that that which they teach will not be superseded by other discoveries which will be more useful to the students? The same students – as Faure reports – that we are trying to prepare for a society which does not as yet exist.

This wish to incorporate new knowledge into that which is taught, new knowledge which is essential to the society of the future, brings with it a need to select and abandon some of what has been traditionally imparted in scholastic institutions. Many teachers are going to have to give up teaching things they included in their material for years, and are going to have to incorporate new things which were not even being talked about when they began teaching.

5 The deterioration of the image of the teacher

In my 1984 paper, 'The image of the teacher in social media', I studied the existence of two contradictory stereotypes used by the media in their treatment of the image of the teacher. On the one hand there exists an idyllic stereotype in which the teacher is presented as a friend and advisor who dedicates him/herself to helping and relating to his/her students and who maintains, even out of the classroom, an attitude of service. This is the subject of such well-known TV series and films as *Fame*, *Lucas Tanner*, *Goodbye Mister Chips*, *Blackboard Jungle*, etc. On the other hand, and this time we are dealing with an image mainly put across in the press, is the more problematic image, linked to situations of physical violence in the classroom, dismissals or ideological clashes, low salaries, lack of materials and facilities, poor heating, etc.

Given the way that teachers work to survive in this profession, the simultaneous presence of two such contradictory stereotypes is no coincidence: it reflects the opposite poles between which hover the self-image of many teachers.

Papers by Honeyford (1982) in England, Gruwez (1983) in France, Vonk (1983) and Veenman (1984) in Holland, Bayer (1984) in Switzerland and Martinez (1984) in Spain, agree in pointing out that the initial training that teachers receive tends to promote the stereotyped ideal presented by the positive pole of the teacher's image. This happens in all circumstances in which a series of norms are established for the teacher to follow, what the teachers *should* do or what the teacher *should* be, without at the same time teaching them how to cope with the day-to-day business of teaching.

Inexperienced teachers are going to find themselves defenceless and disorientated when they discover that the reality of teaching bears no relation to the ideals in accordance with which they have been trained. This is particularly true if their colleagues, in accordance with seniority, present the new teacher with the worst classes, the worst students, the worst timetable, and the worst working conditions. Veenman (1984) used the concept of 'reality shock' to describe this break between the idyllic image and what he called 'the collapse of missionary ideals gained during training because of the hard reality of daily life in the classroom'.

During the first year of teaching, according to Walter's study (1974), 91 per cent find it necessary to seriously revise the idealized image of teaching with which they have been inculcated. After 5 or 6 years of work, according to Amiel (Amiel and Mace-Kradjian 1972) and Stern (1980), the ideal image which the teacher has of his/her work is going to reach a critical point of identity crisis, as Ada Abraham (1985) pointed out, because of the contradiction between the *real* 'I' (what the teacher sees him/herself doing every day in class) and the *ideal* 'I' (what the teacher would *like* to do or what he/she thinks he/she should be doing). The confrontation brought about by this 'identity crisis' as Léon (1980) called it, or 'praxis shock' in the terminology of Veenman (1984), will produce different reactions in teachers which Abraham has classified into four large groups:

1 The predominance of contradictory feelings, without arriving at any practical way of dealing with the conflict between the real and the ideal. The teacher's behaviour will fluctuate, both in his/her teaching and in his/her image of him/herself.
2 The refusal to accept reality due to the teacher's inability to put up with the anxiety thus created. The teacher will resort to different mechanisms of evasion, among which will be those of cutting down on, limiting or making routine that which he/she does as a means of cutting out his/her personal involvement in the task of teaching.
3 The predominance of anxiety when the teacher realizes that he/she lacks the necessary means to put into practice his/her ideals and at the same time wishes to maintain them and to remain personally involved in teaching. Continued comparison between the poverty of the daily practice of teaching and the ideals which the teacher would wish to realize which will lead to yet more anxiety when the teacher reacts hyperactively; trying to compensate for the endemic problems of teaching with his/her own efforts.
4 Another group of teachers react by accepting the conflict as objective reality and give it no more importance than that of looking for adequate answers within the existing framework.

Using the MISPE/60 questionnaire with a sample of 246 EGB (primary) teachers from Málaga and the surrounding area, we studied the four situations described above and obtained the following results.

We found that by far the most common reaction to the 'reality shock' among our sample was a 'balanced' response, through which 34.5 per cent of our teachers accepted the conflict between the ideal and the real and tried to work on this conflict. However, a fairly high number (28 per cent) of these teachers reported feelings of anxiety and self-criticism; and the numbers who said they felt either inhibited or caught between contradictory feelings was 22 and 15 per cent respectively.

PRIMARY FACTORS

Let us now move on to what we have called *primary factors*, including under this heading those factors which directly affect teaching, limit it or produce tension in day-to-day practice. The most obvious contributive factors to teacher burnout will also be revealed.

1   *Materials and working conditions*

A general lack of resources appears as one of the factors in much research. Indeed, many teachers who look forward enthusiastically to a renewal of their activity in the classroom, often find themselves limited by a lack of materials or of the means to obtain them. Many of these teachers complain of the contradiction implicit in the situation whereby, on the one hand, society and those in charge of education are demanding and promoting a renewal in teaching methodology but, on the other hand, do not equip teachers with what they need to put it into practice. This situation, in the long term, will limit the activity of the teacher. On other occasions, as the ILO Report (1981) and the Breuse Report (1984) point out, lack of resources may not be a matter of teaching materials, but a problem of space, poorly preserved buildings, poor quality furniture, inadequate heating, lack of suitable premises, etc.

Apart from a lack of resources, it is worth mentioning that there exist institutional limitations which often interfere in the work of teachers. Both Goble and Porter (1980) and Bayer and Chauvet (1980) make much of the fact that what the teacher does depends to a great extent on the institutional framework in which he/she operates, without being able, as an individual, to modify these limitations, e.g. timetable problems, internal rules, standards laid down by the teaching institution or by the inspecting bodies, the need to set aside time for meetings between members of staff, between staff and students, between staff and the governing body, meetings to discuss examinations, parents' evenings and other activities which may take place in the teaching institution, often make quality teaching difficult.

Under these circumstances, dare I suggest that where quality teaching *does* exist, it is basically the result of the goodwill of teachers who, faced by temptation to give up and resign, look within themselves to find new enthusiasm and energy and, by their efforts, to make up for the lack of facilities? Any improvement attempted by the teacher requires an extra effort in order to get what he/she needs and to move the dead weight which is the institution.

2   *The increase in violence in scholastic institutions*

The most complete data relating to the increase in violence in scholastic institutions is to be found in the USA (National Education Association, 1980). According to these statistics, during the year 1979–80, 113 000 acts of aggression towards teachers took place, which corresponds to 5 per cent of the teachers in state education, an increase of 43 000 cases over 1977–8. As well as these acts of physical aggression towards teachers, some 25 per cent of teachers report having experienced fear of attacks by students.

The 1981 ILO Report makes mention of other reports in which the increase in violence in the classrooms in Israel, the UK, France and Sweden is documented. With respect to Spain, there exist no more accurate data than the fragmentary information offered by the press when these acts of aggression are reported.

If before we defined teacher burnout as the permanent effect of the social and psychological conditions under which teaching is carried out, then the increase of violence in schools is a clear example of one of the mechanisms which produce the phenomenon. In reality, the problem of violence is isolated and sporadic and restricted to a minority. But psychologically the problem is multiplied five-fold, leading to many teachers who have never been attacked and who probably never will be, feeling unsafe and uncertain of where they stand.

According to the 1981 ILO Report, attacks on teachers in secondary schools outnumber those made in primary schools by 5:1, and they are generally carried out by male students and directed at male teachers. In sociological terms, attacks are distributed irregularly according to the situation of the institutions in which they occur, reaching a peak of 15 per cent in schools situated in large urban conurbations, 6 per cent in less densely populated urban areas and only 4 per cent in rural areas. Similarly, there are more attacks in large institutions and those which have an excessive number of students. The impersonal nature of human relationships in these large centres favours the growth of violent action.

Kallen and Colton's study (1980) relates the increase in violence to compulsory schooling. According to their study, which was carried out for UNESCO, young people of working age who are obliged to continue studying against their will, eventually manifest their discontent by acting aggressively against the representatives of the institution in which they see themselves confined.

Finally, it is worth mentioning the relationship between violence within schools and that which exists in society in general, as well as the discrediting of the concept of discipline which, having been criticized as being arbitrary and imposed from the outside on teachers and students alike, has in many cases to date not been replaced by a more just form of keeping order, in which all participate.

3   *Teacher exhaustion and the increasing demands made on teachers*

In Anglo-Saxon bibliography the term 'burnout' appears, in many cases associated with the concept of stress, and has become the focus of much research in the 1980s. Although I have seen it translated as 'exhaustion', it has a meaning much closer to the original when it is translated literally and as an adjective which refers to the teacher – 'burned-out'.

It is often argued that *lack of time* adds to the responsibilities of the teacher and is a principal cause of exhaustion, which may later lead to other problems. Klugman (1979) expressed the problem concisely, calling his paper 'Too many pieces: A study of the fragmentation of the teacher in the elementary classroom'. The idea repeated by all these authors is that teachers are overloaded with work which forces them to 'fragment' their activities as a result of having, at the same time, to operate on several fronts, for example:

- maintain discipline, but be sympathetic and, to some extent, affectionate;
- give individual attention to brighter students who want to proceed more quickly and to slower students;
- maintain a pleasant atmosphere in the classroom;
- plan the work to be done;
- mark examinations and evaluate students;
- help students to plan for the future;
- talk to parents and keep them informed as to the progress of their children;
- organize extra-curricular activities and other public acts;
- attend staff and administrative meetings;
- take care of bureaucratic problems;
- carry out playground and dinner-hour duties and, sometimes, take care of school buses.

Investigation into 'teacher burnout' portrays teachers as overworked professionals forced, because of the demands made upon them – demands which are disproportionate to the means and time they have at their disposal – to do the job badly.

The effects of teacher burnout on the personality of the teacher

Before going into detail I would like to make two points. First, up to now, I have only written about *teacher burnout* and the exhaustion produced by the demands made upon teachers. I have expressed myself in mainly sociological terms and have limited myself to describing the problem. I have tried to describe a general situation, which, to a greater or lesser extent, affects all teachers. However, teachers' reactions to the situation I have described vary greatly and, therefore, the rest of this chapter will concentrate on particulars, given that we cannot generalize about all teachers.

Secondly, we need to particularize what we say when we talk about the effects of teacher burnout on the personality of the teacher. This is particularly true when we attempt to quantify the extent and type of effects which the sources of tension I have mentioned have on teaching activity. Not all the research we have at our disposal makes precisely these qualitative distinctions: some use confusing terminology which is far from specific and speak of 'disadjustment', 'mental health' or 'psychological problems', without going into specific detail about what it is they are referring to, giving at the same time, facts and figures which are not easily compared.

It is very important to make clear that the tension to which teachers are subjected is qualitatively variable and depends on, for example, the type and level of the particular educational institution, the age and experience of the teachers, their sex, etc. For this reason, it is necessary to reject those schemes which establish a simplistic, linear relationship between the complex sociological phenomenon which I have described and the mental health of the teacher. For the same reason, we have to avoid generalized statements.

Figure 1.1 attempts to develop a model which illustrates the link between the different reactions to stress that Abraham describes (see p. 15), and the conditions which generated these reactions. The model shows the relationship, then, between key elements which might promote stress and the four teacher reactions of:

- strong feelings beset by contradictions;
- evasion and routine;
- permanent anxiety;
- happiness, i.e. the achievement of an effective balance between personal resources and occupational demands.

The four distinct ways in which the key elements in teacher stress interact to produce four different reactions are reproduced in Fig. 1.1.

The repercussions on the teacher's personality of the burnout which may result from permanent anxiety are of a wide variety, in which there exist at least 12 stages, of which only the last three clearly refer to the mental health of the teacher. These last are of their nature very important, but of low incidence. Indeed, faced with the situation I have described,

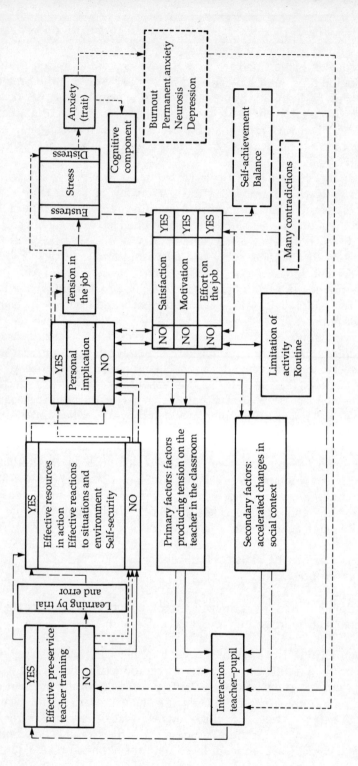

Fig. 1.1   A model to illustrate the link between the four reactions to stress.

teachers adopt different defence mechanisms, e.g. the limiting of activity at work, falling into a routine of absenteeism, mechanisms which decrease the quality of education but which also serve to relieve the tension to which the teacher is subjected. From a statistical point of view, these are the most frequent negative repercussions, much more so than real problems of mental health.

In ascending order, from the point of view of the seriousness of their nature, but in descending order from the point of view of the number of teachers affected, the consequences of teacher burnout could be graded as follows:

1 Feelings of uncertainty or dissatisfaction when faced with the practical problems of teaching, in complete contradiction to the image of the profession which teachers would like to give.
2 Requests for a change of institution as a way of fleeing from different situations.
3 Gradual limiting of the amount of work done as a way of reducing the teacher's own personal involvement in the job.
4 Outright desire to leave the profession (whether realized or not).
5 Absenteeism, as a way of reducing accumulated tension.
6 Stress.
7 Anxiety at times about the job or about what is expected of the teacher.
8 Negative opinions about the teacher's 'self'. Teachers blaming themselves for their inability to succeed in teaching.
9 Neuroses.
10 Depression.
11 Permanent anxiety, cited as cause/effect in various diagnoses of mental illness.

When we come to count the numbers of teachers included in each of these categories, we have to juggle with various figures because of the factors mentioned above (level, sex, years of experience, age, etc.). However, the number of teachers affected varies between 91 per cent of those in their first year who demonstrate feelings of uncertainty (Walter, 1974; Veenman, 1984), and 0.7–0.77 per cent of teachers who, according to our own studies, stop working because of illness, which is diagnosed or accepted officially as being related to mental health. Besides, any attempt to quantify this phenomenon faces problems of disparity caused by the investigative method used and the criteria used to establish the fine line which separates health from illness.

Is there a stress cycle during the scholastic year?

Research carried out in Canada by Hembling and Gilliland (1981) hypothesized about the existence of a stress cycle during the school year.

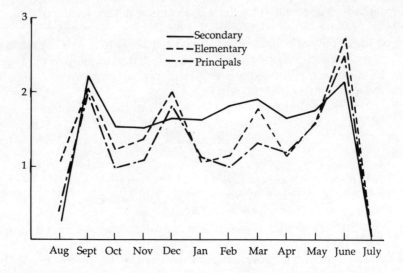

Fig. 1.2 Mean monthly stress perceived by secondary and elementary teachers and principals in Kamloops. From Hembling and Gilliland (1981).

They reported that the highest incidence of stress among teachers occurs at the end of each term and at the end of the school year. This increased stress is due to the tension accumulated during the previous term and the fact that examinations are set at the end of term. Figure 1.2 shows an increase in accumulated stress at the end of term and the importance of school holidays as a means of regaining personal stability.

In an attempt to corroborate the relationship between teachers' stress and sick leave or absenteeism, we have gathered together data on sick leave taken from the records of the Medical Inspection Department of the Regional Education and Science Authority in Málaga, which covers all primary and secondary teachers in the city of Málaga and its province for the year 1985–6 (see Fig. 1.3). Administrative procedures in Spain require all teachers taking more than 3 days' sickness leave to formally register their medical condition with the Medical Inspection Department of their local education authority.

Certainly, those teachers who take sick leave and who are diagnosed as showing symptoms of pathological or medically specific illnesses tend to be heavily represented in stress-related conditions. For example, official statistics on teachers' sickness in Málaga for 1985–6 show the following startling raw figures:

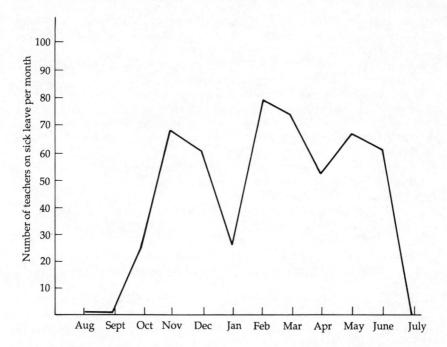

Fig. 1.3 Official sick leave of primary and secondary school teachers in Málaga and province, school year 1985–6. From Franco and Esteve (1987). Note that the last week of April was a holiday for all teachers.

- 12.5 per cent of 7321 teachers took sick leave during the year for an average of 34 days each; and
- of these 899 teachers 11 per cent were diagnosed as suffering from neuro-psychiatric conditions, 15 per cent from respiratory or cardiovascular problems, and 9 per cent had complaints affecting the digestive system.

Stress in teaching might, it seems, be costly in both human and economic terms.

References

Abraham, A. (1985). *Modele multi-dimensionnel pour l'étude du soi et du soi collectif.* Éditions Scientifiques et Psychologiques: Issy-les-Moulineaux.

Amiel, R. and Mace-Kradjian, G. (1972). Quelques données épidemiologiques sur la psychosociologie et la psychopathologie du monde enseignant. *Annales Médico-Psychologiques* **3** (Octobre), 321–53.

Bayer, E. (1984). Práctica pedagógica y representaciones de la identidad profesional del enseñante. In Esteve, J. M. (ed.), *Profesores en conflicto*. Narcea: Madrid.

Bayer, E. and Chauvet, N. (1980). *Libertés et contraintes de l'exercise pedagogique*. Faculté de Psychologie et Sciences de l'Éducation: Géneve.

Blase, J. J. (1982). A social-psychological grounded theory of teacher stress and burnout. *Educational Administration Quarterly* 18(4), 93–113.

Breuse, E. (1984). Identificación de las fuentes de tensión en el trabajo profesional del enseñante. In Esteve, J. M. (ed.), *Profesores en conflicto*. Narcea: Madrid.

Cole, M. (1985). A crisis of identity: Teachers in times of political and economical change. *Coloquio Internacional sobre Función Docente y Salud Mental*. Universidad de Salamanca: Salamanca.

Esteve, J. M. (1984) L'image des enseignants dans les moyens de communication de masse. *European Journal of Teacher Education* 7(2), 203–9.

Faure, E. (1973). *Aprender a ser*. Alianza: Madrid.

Franco, S. and Esteve, J. M. (1987). La profesión docente: un estudio sobre la salud y el absentismo del profesorado. Unpublished thesis, University of Málaga, Spain.

Goble, N. M. and Porter, J. F. (1980). *La cambiante función del profesor*. Narcea: Madrid.

Gruwez, J. (1983). La formation des maîtres en France. *European Journal of Teacher Education* 6(3), 281–9.

Hembling, D. W. and Gilliland, B. (1981). Is there an identifiable stress cycle in the school year? *The Alberta Journal of Educational Research* 27(4), 324–30.

Honeyford, R. (1982). *Starting Teaching*. Guilford: London.

ILO (1981). *Emploi et conditions de travail des enseignants*. Bureau Internationale du Travail: Géneve.

Kallen, D. and Colton, S. (1980). *Educational Developments in Europe and North America Since 1960*. UNESCO: Paris.

Klugman, E. (1979). *Too Many Pieces: A Study of Teacher Fragmentation in the Elementary School*. Wheelock: Boston.

Léon, A. (1980). La profesión docente: motivaciones, actualización de conocimientos y promoción. In Debesse, M. and Mialaret, G. (eds.), *La función docente*. Oikos-Tau: Barcelona.

Martinez, A. (1984). El perfeccionamiento de la función didáctica como vía de disminución de tensiones en el docente. In Esteve, J. M. (ed.), *Profesores en conflicto*. Narcea: Madrid.

Merazzi, C. (1983). Apprendre á vivre les conflits: une tâche de la formation des enseignants. *European Journal of Teacher Education* 6(2), 101–6.

Mitter, W. (1985). Goal aspects of teacher education. *European Journal of Teacher Education* 8(3), 273–82.

National Education Association (1980). Teacher's problems. *Today's education*. Nov.–Dec. 1979, p. 5 and Sept.–Oct. 1980, p. 21.

OECD (1983). *Compulsory Schooling in a Changing World*. OECD: Paris.

Ranjard, P. (1984). *Les enseignants persécutés*. Robert Jauze: Paris.

Stern, W. A. (1980). *Teacher Absenteeism at the Secondary School Level*. Michigan State University: Detroit.

Toffler, A. (1970). *Future Shock*. Bodley Head: London.

Veenman, S. (1984). Perceived problems of beginning teachers. *Review of Educational Research* 54(2), 143–78.

Vonk, J. H. C. (1983). Problems of the beginning teacher. *European Journal of Teacher Education* 6(2), 133–50.

Walter, H. (1974). Auf der Suche nach dem Selbstverständnis. In Ipfling, H. J. (ed.), *Verunsicher-te Lehrer*? Ehrenwirth: München.

2 DEFINING STRESS

Comment: Disruptive pupils drive teachers from schools.

Disruptive pupils might well drive teachers from school, we don't really know. But what this newspaper headline (to an article about the conference on which this book is based) certainly does illustrate, is the kind of over-simplistic and mono-causal explanations of how teachers respond to their working conditions which are to be found in the press and popular opinion. Such explanations are usually anecdotal, linear and present tidy versions of a messy reality.

Discussion of teaching and stress is plagued by this sort of mythology. So, teachers are not only depicted as the guilty victims of their own emotional inadequacies but, also, the link between the conditions of teaching and how teachers deal with their work is seen in simplistic terms of stimulus-response. Certain episodes and events provoke certain reactions. In fact, as the following paper by Kyriacou shows, both the nature and the source of stress in teaching are complex and contradictory. To begin with, the problem of pupil management does not seem to be a major source of stress for most teachers. Of course, this is not to say that such work is not sometimes difficult and taxing; but teachers would appear to perceive pupil management as a normal rather than necessarily stressful part of their work. Also, while teachers report feeling fairly high levels of occupational stress, the incidence of stress-related illness in teaching is fairly low. Both these observations point to the massive degree of subjectivity in definitions of stress in teaching and in the source of this stress. Not all teachers will find the same episode or set of circumstances stressful; the conditions certain teachers subjectively define as stressful are not static but shifting, and not all stress will be dysfunctional.

THE NATURE AND PREVALENCE OF TEACHER STRESS

Chris Kyriacou

Over the last 10 years there has been a steady increase in interest in occupational stress among schoolteachers ('teacher stress'), such that the level of discussion and research currently taking place makes teacher stress one of the major areas of attention within education (see Dunham, 1986 and Kyriacou, 1987, for reviews of research over the last decade). While great strides have been made in understanding the nature of stress in teaching and the major sources of stress facing teachers, we still have some way to go in developing strategies and techniques for reducing levels of stress in schools.

First, however, we need to be clear about what is meant by the term 'teacher stress'. One of the main problems facing those attempting to get to grips with the various writings on teacher stress is that the term has been used in a number of different ways. My own preferred definition is that teacher stress refers to the experience by teachers of unpleasant emotions such as anger, tension, frustration, anxiety, depression and nervousness, resulting from aspects of their work as teachers. In essence, I am defining stress as an unpleasant emotional state. This may be contrasted with others who have, for example, defined stress either in terms of the nature of the pressures and demands facing teachers, or in terms of an excess of pressures and demands on teachers over their ability to cope with the pressures and demands (for examples of other definitions of teacher stress, see Blase, 1986; Payne and Fletcher, 1983; Tellenback *et al.*, 1983). Overall, it is teacher stress seen as an unpleasant emotional state that is the most widely used definition of this term (for a more detailed discussion, see Kyriacou and Sutcliffe, 1978a).

In recent years, however, a related term has begun to receive substantial attention – 'teacher burnout' (a somewhat alarming image is conjured up for teachers who first come across this term with no explanation for its meaning). Teacher burnout refers to a state of mental, emotional and attitudinal exhaustion in teachers which results from a prolonged experience of stress (see Cunningham, 1983; Farber, 1984). Such teachers are still able to function as teachers, but they have largely lost their commitment and enthusiasm for their work, and this inevitably shows in aspects of their job performance. One possible signal of this would be a teacher who arrives at school on the last day of term with his caravan already hitched to the back of his car!

Why do teachers experience stress?

In essence stress is primarily the body's natural emotional and physio-logical reaction to the perception of danger in one's environment; in classic psychological terms, the body is being prepared for 'fight' or 'flight'. What is evident now, is that such a perception of danger is by no means limited to physical danger, as it presumably was in early evolution. Rather, the perception of threat to one's self-esteem and mental well-being in general is also a potent trigger of this emotional state. Teachers are faced daily with many and various demands; if the teacher *perceives* that meeting certain demands will be difficult or impossible, and that failure to do so will threaten his mental or physical well-being, then the teacher is very likely to experience stress. It is worth noting that such demands may well be self-imposed as well as imposed by others, just as the judgements about meeting the demands successfully may be based on the teacher's own criteria as well as those of others.

Almost all models of teacher stress acknowledge the central role of the teacher's perception of his circumstances as the trigger for stress (e.g. Payne and Fletcher, 1983; Tellenback *et al.*, 1983), and this goes some way to explaining why teachers in apparently similar circumstances appear to experience different levels of stress. Presumably, those teachers who *perceive* the circumstances as more threatening, are the teachers who experience greater levels of stress. In one sense, stress is in the eye of the beholder. This is of course not to say that an objective assessment of the level of difficulty facing a particular teacher is neither here nor there, but merely to clarify why the nature and type of job demands are not the sole unequivocal predictors of the level of stress the teacher will experience.

Meeting job demands is very dependent on the skills and strategies teachers have and the degree of control they thereby have in dealing with their circumstances. Much research now shows that the degree of control teachers feel they have over the demands made upon them is of crucial importance. Where teachers feel they have some control over the frequency and nature of the demands made upon them and over the ability to deal successfully with these demands, stress is likely to be minimized. One interesting caveat to this, is that there is now evidence emerging that teachers with a personality disposition to see their life circumstances as in general being under their control are also less likely to experience stress (e.g. Kyriacou and Sutcliffe, 1979; McIntyre, 1984).

Why is teacher stress a problem?

Clearly, the major concern with teacher stress in schools is that a pro-longed experience of stress can precipitate both mental and physical ill-health (Armes, 1985; Kyriacou and Pratt, 1985; Stratford *et al.*, 1986). While there is much evidence that stress at work appears to be implicated in the ill-health of many teachers, the relationship between occupational stress and subsequent ill-health is a complex one (see Cox and Brockley, 1984; Stratford *et al.*, 1986; Kyriacou, 1980a) – a point which will be developed in the next section of this chapter.

Teacher stress is also a problem in schools because of its effect on job performance. This can include teacher absences, taken to avoid stress or resulting from stress-precipitated ill-health, a lowered level of job satis-faction and commitment (as evidenced in studies of teacher burnout) and even an impaired quality of classroom teaching (in the sense that a teacher's rapport and relationship with pupils can easily be adversely affected if the teacher is experiencing a high level of stress). Whereas in the early 1970s much of the concern also focused on the number of teachers leaving the profession through stress, as employment prospects elsewhere for ex-teachers became more difficult, this trend appears now to have led to many teachers remaining in the profession who would in the past have left. Such teachers may be prone to burnout and account for some of the increase in the number of teachers taking early retirement through ill-health (Owen, 1984).

How widespread is teacher stress?

Estimating the extent of teacher stress is difficult because there is no widely accepted objective measure of stress. While a variety of objective measures have been used, each is subject to major shortcomings and limitations. Physiological measures, for example, are easily influenced by factors other than stress or by differences between individuals in how they reflect stress. Sutcliffe and Whitfield (1976), for example, attempted to identify when teachers were making stressful decisions during a lesson by monitoring their heart rate, only to find that their data largely reflected teachers' physical activity. Behavioural measures such as absenteeism, leaving the profession or ill-health are also prone to influence by too many other factors. The link with ill-health is particularly interesting in this respect, in that levels of stress-related illnesses appear to be no higher in teaching than in many other professions. It is likely, however, that the periodic school holidays may well enable teachers to recover physically and mentally from periods of stress and thereby mitigate any ill-health that would otherwise have occurred in a way that is not available to those in most professions.

As a result of the difficulties in obtaining objective measures of teacher stress, much of the research on estimating the extent of teacher stress has relied on some form of self-report questionnaire. A variety of such instruments has developed over the years (see Hiebert and Farber, 1984; Kyriacou, 1987). The most straightforward example is a simple self-report, one-item rating scale as used in my own studies, where teachers in comprehensive schools in England were asked to respond to the question 'In general, how stressful do you find being a teacher?' by using one of five categories: 'not at all stressful', 'mildly stressful', 'moderately stress-ful', 'very stressful' and 'extremely stressful' (Kyriacou, 1980b). In these studies, I found that about 25 per cent of the teachers responded by using the categories 'very stressful' or 'extremely stressful'. This simple type of survey has been used in numerous studies all over the world, in this form or with some minor adaptations (e.g. Galloway *et al.*, 1987; Knutton and Mycroft, 1986; Laughlin, 1984). Two examples of more complex measures are the Teacher Event Stress Inventory (TESI) developed by Pratt (1978) and the Teacher Stress Inventory (TSI) developed by Fimian (1984), both of which attempt to incorporate information about the frequency and strength of particular sources of stress into the inventory. In addition, there are a number of measures of stress not specific to teachers which have been employed, the most commonly used being the Maslach Burnout Inventory (MBI) (see Maslach and Jackson, 1981) which attempts to assess the respondent's emotional and attitudinal state using more generalized items.

Surveys indicate that teachers report experiencing stress at work more than the majority of other professions (other professions with typically high self-report ratings include social workers, managers, junior hospital doctors, nurses, the clergy, journalists, air traffic controllers, the police and actors), although it must be acknowledged that survey data compar-ing professions is surprisingly sparse and subject to a particular degree of caution. Nevertheless, despite the various shortcomings of such self-report data, the large number of studies reported of teacher stress do indeed suggest that teaching is one of the most stressful of the professions.

What are the major sources of stress facing teachers?

One of the aspects of teacher stress that has been extremely well re-searched is that of identifying the sources of such stress (Kyriacou, 1987). Whereas most of the studies rely on data obtained from questionnaire surveys (e.g. Laughlin, 1984), there have in recent years been many studies making use of interview data (e.g. Dewe, 1986) and case-study designs (e.g. Freeman, 1987).

Overall, the sources of stress identified appear to fall into six major categories:

• poor motivation in pupils,

- pupil indiscipline,
- poor working conditions,
- time pressures,
- low status, and
- conflicts with colleagues.

Pupils' poor attitudes towards school and their lack of motivation has consistently been identified as a major source of stress in numerous studies (e.g. Laughlin, 1984; Payne and Furnham, 1987). Indeed, it is probably the effort involved in teaching such pupils on a regular basis that forms the single most important source of stress. While actual indiscipline is also a major area of stress, indiscipline by pupils can be dealt with competently by most teachers most of the time without undue stress (obviously in some schools and for some teachers this may not be the case); the problem of poorly motivated pupils, however, is a more consistent and in some ways harder state of affairs to deal with.

Indiscipline as a source of stress has been widely discussed (e.g. Dunham, 1984; Galloway *et al.*, 1982; Laslett and Smith, 1984). Particular attention has been paid to the way in which a tense and highly unpleasant exchange between a teacher and a pupil can take place almost before the participants have realized how the situation arose. Such exchanges can be extremely stressful at the time, although in most cases they are quickly over.

Poor working conditions include such problems as inadequate equipment, poor staffroom facilities, and teaching at a split-site school (e.g. Dewe, 1986; Dunham, 1984; Kyriacou and Sutcliffe, 1978b). Time pressures refer to the general level of demands made on teachers within very short periods of time; indeed, the variety of demands made on a teacher in a typical school day, often with tight deadlines attached to them, make this aspect of teaching a major area of stress (e.g. Dewe, 1986; Laughlin, 1984).

Low status refers to teachers' perceptions that their profession is held in low esteem by the wider society; this is in part reflected by the level of salaries for teachers and how teaching is discussed by the wider society, particularly through the media. In the United Kingdom, there is little doubt that the recent pay dispute and the criticism of teachers in some newspapers contributed to lowered morale within the profession. This is of great concern, since professional self-esteem appears to act as a buffer between stress at work and the likelihood of a precipitating stress-related illness. Some recent studies have indicated that undermining teachers' professional self-esteem and identity makes teachers much more vulnerable to teacher burnout (e.g. Kremer and Hofman, 1985).

Conflict with colleagues has also been reported as a major area of stress (e.g. Dewe, 1986; Moracco *et al.*, 1982). Such conflicts can range from purely academic disagreements to those arising from the exercise of managerial direction. In the close-knit world of schools, such conflicts can easily escalate if not dealt with skilfully.

While these six areas have emerged as the most commonly identified sources of stress, a number of important caveats need to be borne in mind. First, for any individual teacher, almost any aspect of his/her work may result in extreme stress, even if that particular source of stress is one rarely of concern to other teachers. Each teacher has his/her own unique stress profile and, in discussing sources of stress in general, it is important not to lose sight of the individual teacher's concerns (Kyriacou, 1986).

Secondly, there are many changes taking place in schools, so that our understanding of the current major sources of stress needs to be based on up-to-date information. In the United Kingdom, for example, recent changes in the school curriculum (ranging from introducing more science in primary schools to new forms of assessment in the secondary schools) make it very likely that meeting the demands stemming from curriculum changes will emerge as a major area of stress in schools. In addition, there are areas of major stress which have appeared in a number of studies, but not consistently so; of these, the most important appear to be the lack of promotion opportunities, the need to maintain standards, pressure from parents, covering for absent colleagues, and being involved in the reorganization of schools.

Thirdly, there are particular groups of teachers which can usefully be looked at separately in order to gain additional insights into their sources of stress. For example, studies of those in managerial positions, such as heads of departments (Dunham, 1984), deputy heads (Knutton and Mycroft, 1986) and headteachers (Dunham, 1984), have highlighted the stress stemming from their managerial role: role conflict, motivating colleagues, fears of being unpopular, the exercise of responsibility, and difficulties over administrative work. Studies of teachers concerned directly with pastoral care (e.g. Freeman, 1987) have highlighted the difficulties of discharging their role to their own satisfaction, in part because of the nature of trying to help pupils with problems and in part because such teachers have to discharge this role alongside other teaching demands. Studies of student teachers (e.g. Hart, 1987) typically highlight concerns over the adequacy of their classroom teaching (both in terms of academic content and in terms of maintaining discipline), and the process of being evaluated by their college supervisor. While a number of studies have presented data focusing on primary schools (e.g. Galloway et al., 1987), secondary schools (e.g. Payne and Furnham, 1987) and special schools (e.g. Pont and Reid, 1985), surprisingly few differences in the major types of stress have emerged from comparing teachers in these three groups.

Conclusions

There is little doubt that teaching in schools is one of the more stressful professions, and the nature of the demands made on teachers in their work means that this is likely to remain a stressful profession for many years to come. We now have a good understanding of both the nature of stress and the major sources of stress facing teachers. Such an understanding can provide a useful basis for developing strategies which individual teachers can apply to reduce their own stress, and for changes in school organizational and managerial practices which will also contribute to reduced levels of stress.

References

Armes, D. (1985). *The Unhappiest Profession.* Report for the Teachers' Joint Committee (AMMA, NAS/UWT, NUT) (available from the author, 5 Ambleside Avenue, Bradford BD9 5HX, England).

Blase, J. J. (1986). A qualitative analysis of sources of teacher stress: Consequences for performance. *American Educational Research Journal* **23**, 13–40.

Cox, T. and Brockley, T. (1984). The experience and effects of stress in teachers. *British Educational Research Journal* **10**, 83–7.

Cunningham, W. G. (1983). Teacher burnout – solutions for the 1980s: A review of the literature. *Urban Review* **15**, 37–51.

Dewe, P. J. (1986). An investigation into the causes and consequences of teacher stress. *New Zealand Journal of Educational Studies* **21**, 145–57.

Dunham, J. (1984). *Stress in Teaching.* Croom Helm: London.

Dunham, J. (1986). A decade of stress in teaching research in the United Kingdom (1976–86). *School Organisation and Management Abstracts* **5**, 161–73.

Farber, B. A. (1984). Stress and burnout in suburban teachers. *Journal of Educational Research* **77**, 325–31.

Fimian, M. J. (1984). The development of an instrument to measure occupational stress in teachers: The Teacher Stress Inventory. *Journal of Occupational Psychology* **57**, 277–93.

Freeman, A. (1987). Pastoral care and teacher stress. *Pastoral Care in Education* **5**, 22–8.

Galloway, D., Ball, T., Blomfield, D. and Seyd, R. (1982). *Schools and Disruptive Pupils.* Longman: London.

Galloway, D., Panckhurst, F., Boswell, K., Boswell, C. and Green, K. (1987). Sources of stress for class teachers in New Zealand primary schools. *Pastoral Care in Education* **5**, 28–36.

Hart, N. I. (1987). Student teachers' anxieties: Four measured factors and their relationships to pupil disruption in class. *Educational Research* **29**, 12–18.

Hiebert, B. and Farber, I. (1984). Teacher stress: A literature survey with a view to surprises. *Canadian Journal of Education* **9**, 14–27.

Knutton, S. and Mycroft, A. (1986). Stress and the deputy head. *School Organization* **6**, 49–59.

Kremer, L. and Hofman, J. E. (1985). Teachers' professional identity and burn-out. *Research in Education* **34**, 89–95.

Kyriacou, C. (1980a). Stress, health and schoolteachers: A comparison with other professions. *Cambridge Journal of Education* **10**, 154–9.

Kyriacou, C. (1980b). Sources of stress among British teachers: The contribution of job factors and personality factors. In Cooper, C. L. and Marshall, J. (eds), *White Collar and Professional Stress*. John Wiley: Chichester.

Kyriacou, C. (1986). *Effective Teaching in Schools*. Basil Blackwell: Oxford.

Kyriacou, C. (1987). Teacher stress and burnout: An international review. *Educational Research* **29**, 146–52.

Kyriacou, C. and Pratt, J. (1985). Teacher stress and psychoneurotic symptoms. *British Journal of Educational Psychology* **55**, 61–4.

Kyriacou, C. and Sutcliffe, J. (1978a). A model of teacher stress. *Educational Studies* **4**, 1–6.

Kyriacou, C. and Sutcliffe, J. (1978b). Teacher stress: Prevalence, sources and symptoms. *British Journal of Educational Psychology* **48**, 159–67.

Kyriacou, C. and Sutcliffe, J. (1979). A note on teacher stress and locus of control. *Journal of Occupational Psychology* **52**, 227–8.

Laslett, R. and Smith, C. (1984). *Effective Classroom Management*. Croom Helm: London.

Laughlin, A. (1984). Teacher stress in an Australian setting: The role of bio-graphical mediators. *Educational Studies* **10**, 7–22.

McIntyre, T. C. (1984). The relationship between locus of control and teacher burnout. *British Journal of Educational Psychology* **54**, 235–8.

Maslach, C. and Jackson, S. E. (1981). The measurement of experienced burnout. *Journal of Occupational Behaviour* **2**, 99–113.

Moracco, J., Danford, D. and D'Arienzo, R. V. (1982). The factorial validity of the teacher occupational stress factor questionnaire. *Educational and Psychological Measurement* **42**, 275–83.

Owen, W. (1984). The cost of teacher stress. Unpublished paper, Monash University, Faculty of Education.

Payne, M. A. and Furnham, A. (1987). Dimensions of occupational stress in West Indian secondary school teachers. *British Journal of Educational Psychology* **57**, 141–50.

Payne, R. L. and Fletcher, B. C. (1983). Job demands, supports and constraints as predictors of psychological strain among schoolteachers. *Journal of Vocational Behavior* **22**, 136–47.

Pont, H. and Reid, G. (1985). Stress in special education: The need for trans-actional data. *Scottish Educational Review* **17**, 107–15.

Pratt, J. (1978). Perceived stress among teachers: The effects of age and back-ground of children taught. *Educational Review* **30**, 3–14.

Stratford, B., Eggleston, J. F., Brown, D. and Herbert, M. (1986). Stress related diseases in teachers (with particular reference to special schools). Unpublished report, University of Nottingham, School of Education and School of Medicine.

Sutcliffe, J. and Whitfield, R. (1976). Decision making in the classroom: An initial report. *Research Intelligence* **2**, 14–19.

Tellenback, S., Brenner, S. and Löfgren, H. (1983). Teacher stress: Exploratory model building. *Journal of Occupational Psychology* **56**, 19–33.

3 RESEARCHING STRESS

Comment: Is it just me, or . . . ?

We have already suggested in our introduction that the concept of stress is inherently problematic. Inevitably, therefore, research on stress is also beset by dangers.

These dangers arise partly from the fact that stress can only be experienced subjectively. So there is an immediate problem that researchers may impose their own subjective perception and understanding on others' subjective experience yet think it to constitute a 'scientific' objectivity. This problem is exacerbated by the complexity of the phenomenon of stress, wherein a wide range of factors may be at work – in different ways with different individuals – in an ever-changing dynamic process. Moreover, cause can easily be confused with effect: 'Do I drink too much because I'm under stress, or am I under stress because I drink too much?'

Research thrives on tidy categorizations and a separating out of factors, but these processes may shatter the complex, interactive reality of a subjectively experienced, dynamic phenomenon like stress. All these dangers in researching stress are the greater when the samples studied are small. Nevertheless, we need to know more about the causes and effects of stress. The three research papers that follow represent contrasting attempts to take our understanding forward.

Chakravorty brings a medical perspective to a study of 33 teachers whose long-term sickness absence arose from psychiatric disorders in most cases attributable in part to stress. Capel attempts to identify the significant variables in the job of teaching that relate to the levels of stress experienced, while Freeman compares the levels and kinds of stress in two teaching situations.

While the scale of these studies makes generalization unwise, their findings do suggest important possibilities for further, more extensive study.

STRESS AND BURNOUT IN SECONDARY SCHOOL TEACHERS: SOME CAUSAL FACTORS

Susan Capel

Introduction

Research into stress has grown steadily over the last few decades. However, burnout, which has been identified as one type of chronic response to the cumulative, long-term negative impact of work stress (Blase, 1982), rather than a short-term, but more intense level of stress, only became a topic for research more recently. It was first identified by Freudenberger in 1974, and since then research has enabled this phenomenon to be identified and distinguished from stress. The 43 teachers surveyed by Blase (1982) indicated that burnout was a result of excessive work stress over extended periods of time. Begley (1982) studied 124 special education administrators to determine causes of burnout and found that professionals experiencing continued stress and strain due to unrelenting work demands were particularly subject to burnout.

I became interested in the phenomenon of burnout after I realized that one of the reasons I had left the teaching profession to return to full-time study was because I was burned-out by teaching. While I was studying it became apparent that many other people had also returned to full-time education because they were burned-out by their jobs. I attended several different courses and read as much as I could about stress and burnout. The more I learned about these two things, the more I became interested and the more I wanted to become involved in research in the area. I started research in the area with my Ph.D. dissertation, which looked at factors causing burnout among athletic trainers (sports physiotherapists), as this profession seemed one in which burnout was particularly prevalent, and one which several of my friends had left because they had become burned-out. Athletic trainers are responsible to a large number of people – the doctor, the coach and the athlete – all of whom may make different demands on them. The athletic trainer's time is largely dictated by other people, and they have very little control over their working lives (Capel, 1986). All these factors could contribute to burnout.

This study was followed by research into the effects of role conflict and role ambiguity on burnout in high school teacher/coaches in the NW United States (Capel *et al.*, 1987). In the United States school teaching and the coaching of school teams are two distinct roles, which are often incompatible. This may, therefore, cause great problems of role conflict and role ambiguity for an individual holding both jobs. On returning to

England I wanted to look more into if and why secondary school teachers become burned-out. I selected secondary schools because I had been a secondary school teacher, and I am now involved in teacher preparation for the secondary age range and, therefore, I have much more experience of the problems that teachers in secondary schools may face.

DEFINITIONS USED IN THE STUDY

For the purposes of this study, the following definitions are used; stress, burnout, locus of control, role conflict and role ambiguity. *Stress* has been defined as being a process that involves the perception of a substantial imbalance between environmental demand and response capability, under conditions where failure to meet demand is perceived as having important consequences and is responded to with increased levels of state anxiety (Martens, 1982). *Burnout* is defined as a reaction to job-related stress that varies in nature with the intensity and duration of the stress itself, which may result in workers becoming emotionally detached from their jobs and may ultimately lead them to leave their jobs altogether (Daley, 1979). *Locus of control* is defined here as people's general perception of the contingent relationship between their behaviour and events which follow their behaviour. People with an external locus of control believe that events are only occasionally contingent on their own actions, often occurring because of fate or the interaction of powerful others. People with an internal locus of control believe that events are almost always contingent on their own actions (Rotter, 1966). *Role conflict* is defined as the degree of perceived conflict between expected role behaviours and *role ambiguity* is the lack of clear information regarding expectations associated with a particular role, the method of fulfilling a known role expectation and/or the consequences of role performance (Kahn *et al.*, 1964).

CAUSES AND CONSEQUENCES OF STRESS AND BURNOUT IN TEACHERS

Much has been said about stress in the other papers in this volume, and studies have indicated teaching to be a very stressful occupation (Dunham, 1976; Kyriacou and Sutcliffe, 1978a, b). Some of these teachers experiencing stress will also become burned-out. Some studies have indicated a relationship between teaching and burnout (Begley, 1982; Schwab, 1981).

A few of the conditions that precipitate burnout have been identified. Lawrenson and McKinnon (1982) studied 33 teachers of emotionally disturbed children and found that being aware of the stressful nature of the job was important in helping prevent burnout. A study by Nagy

(1982), of individual factors related to burnout, found that type A personality, workaholism and perceptions of working environment contributed to burnout, but none were good predictors of its occurrence.

Numerous organizational and situational causes have been implicated in causing burnout. Pines and Aronson (1981) indicated that different organizational environments significantly affected staff burnout rates within organizations. Very similar organizations have been found to have significantly different levels of burnout and, therefore, the organizational environment may often be the crucial element in determining the level of burnout. Pines (1982b) identified dimensions of the organizational environment which have been found to play an important part in preventing or promoting burnout. These included (a) the psychological – including cognitive (e.g. autonomy, variety, overload), and emotional (e.g. significance, actualization, growth) – (b) the physical (e.g. fixed structures, space, lighting and flexibility to change fixed features of the environment), (c) the social (e.g. number of and problems and relationships with pupils, support and relationships with other staff and feedback and support from superiors and administrators), and (d) the work environment (e.g. bureaucracy, various administrative rules, regulations and influences and the individual's role in the organization – conflict, ambiguity and overload). Westerhouse (1979), in a study of 141 teachers, and Schwab (1981), in a study of 469 classroom teachers, both showed that role conflict and role ambiguity were significantly related to burnout. Again, as with individual factors, organizational factors alone do not seem to explain burnout to a large extent.

Cooley and Savicki (1981) concluded from a study of 40 teachers that individual, social–psychological and organizational factors were all strongly associated with burnout and, therefore, considering these three types of factors together would help explain burnout better than considering one of the factors alone. Fielding (1982) found that teachers with negative attitudes and beliefs about students, an external locus of control and intolerance of ambiguity reported more burnout than other teachers. He also reported that the relationship between personality and burnout was stronger in schools with a negative work climate than in schools with a positive work climate. Zabel and Zabel (1982) studied 100 teachers from different categories of exceptionality and found that, among other things, young, less experienced teachers experienced higher levels of burnout. Also, those receiving more support from administrators, fellow teachers and parents, and more external support were less burned-out than other teachers. Support, encouragement and various administrative practices were also related to burnout. Burnout is, therefore, a complex issue, and an interactional approach to its study needs to be adopted in line with the approach adopted to study stress.

Most researchers agree that burnout results in a state of physical, mental and emotional exhaustion (Pines, 1982a), with high emotional exhaustion, high depersonalization and low personal accomplishment being the three most common symptoms. One isolated symptom does not necessarily imply burnout, but a number of symptoms occurring simultaneously may indicate that burnout exists.

The result of burnout is that it detracts from the quality of teaching. Studies have shown that burned-out teachers gave significantly less information and less praise, showed less acceptance of their pupils' ideas, and interacted less frequently with them (Mancini *et al.*, 1982, 1984).

Thus, burnout can have a negative impact on the teachers themselves and on the pupils they teach. It is therefore important to eliminate, or at least reduce, burnout in teachers. In order to attempt to reduce burnout for one individual, factors increasing stress and the possibility of burnout specific to that individual in that specific environment need to be examined. However, to do this, it is also important to identify potential causes of stress and burnout common across professions, to the teaching profession generally, and one school specifically, so that steps can be taken to reduce these risk elements.

PURPOSE OF THE STUDY

The specific purpose of this study was to evaluate different factors which contribute to increased stress and burnout in teachers in four secondary schools. Eight factors were included, and these are shown in Table 3.1.

WHY EACH INDEPENDENT VARIABLE WAS INCLUDED IN THE STUDY

Previous research has shown that individual, social–psychological and organizational variables all contribute to stress and burnout, and if considered together in an interactional approach, a larger amount of stress and burnout can be explained than if only one is considered. It was therefore considered important to have an interactional approach with individual, social–psychological and organizational variables included in the study. These eight variables were chosen because they seemed to be the most crucial in helping to explain this phenomenon.

The individual variables of fewer years' teaching experience and fewer years at present position were considered important because it seems likely that those teachers who remain in teaching longer are those who have survived stress and burnout and so remained in the job (Zabel and Zabel, 1982). Likewise, in a new position, a teacher is likely to be experiencing more stress because of uncertainty about the environment, routines and expected behaviours, and there are many new challenges, etc. Overload has been shown to be an important factor in causing stress

Table 3.1   The eight factors included to determine their influence on stress and burnout in teachers.

Individual (demographic) variables
Total number of years as a teacher
Total number of years at present position
Number of times per week school work taken home to do

Social–psychological variables
Role conflict
Role ambiguity
Locus of control

Organizational (situational) variables
Number of hours per week involved with extracurricular activities
Number of different classes taught per week.

and burnout and, therefore, taking school work home to do more often, being heavily involved in extracurricular activities, and teaching more different classes per week (because of the added preparation for a greater variety of lessons) could be important factors in increasing a teacher's work load, and could lead to a situation where a teacher does not have enough time away from the job to relax and recover and be refreshed ready to start the next day. Higher role conflict, higher role ambiguity, and having an external locus of control have been shown to be important in other studies (Fielding, 1982; Schwab, 1981). Role conflict and role ambiguity are likely to be factors affecting teachers, especially in periods of uncertainty – in the profession in general, as well as in individual schools.

The four schools selected for the study were chosen because of personal contacts in the schools who could distribute and collect the question-naires sent to the teachers in those schools. They were also selected because they covered a spectrum of schools – different in size, age range of pupils in the school, catchment area, ethnic and social backgrounds of the pupils, etc. Because the four schools were very different, this in itself may have caused differences in the amount and causes of stress and burnout among the staff. A follow-up survey is being undertaken to include all middle, high and upper schools in Bedfordshire (total = 80 schools), to look at differences in the amount and causes of stress and burnout experienced by teachers working in these different types of schools, as this was not undertaken in the present study.

HYPOTHESES

With a knowledge of stress in general and burnout in particular, it was hypothesized that teachers with fewer years' total teaching experience and fewer years at present position, who took school work home to do more frequently, had higher role conflict and role ambiguity in the job, had an external locus of control, were involved more hours per week in extracurricular activities and taught more different classes per week would experience more stress and burnout.

Method and results*

A total of 160 teachers in four secondary schools were sent a questionnaire in September 1985 containing scales to measure the dependent variables of stress and burnout, along with scales to measure the independent variables included in the study (as listed in the previous paragraph). These scales measured the perceived levels and symptoms of stress (Kyriacou and Sutcliffe, 1978a), perceived level of total burnout, frequency and strength of total burnout and the subscales of emotional exhaustion, depersonalization and personal accomplishment (Maslach Burnout Inventory: Maslach and Jackson, 1981), perceived levels of role conflict and role ambiguity (Role Questionnaire: Rizzo et al., 1970), and locus of control (Rotter Internal–External Locus of Control Scale: Rotter, 1966). All scales used were valid and reliable. They are the most widely used scales in research in their respective areas and are considered the most appropriate scales for a study such as this. There were also questions about teaching experience and current teaching position. These questions obtained data about total number of years' teaching experience, number of years at present position, number of times per week school work is taken home to do, number of hours per week involved with extracurricular activities and number of different classes taught per week. Of the 160 teachers involved in the study, 78 (56.5 per cent) returned their questionnaire.

Results showed that levels of stress and burnout among teachers in this sample were medium or low. A total of 19 and 49 per cent reported medium levels of stress and burnout, and 81 and 51 per cent reported low levels of stress and burnout, respectively. Low levels of role conflict and role ambiguity were also reported. Further, 63 per cent of the sample reported an internal locus of control, and 37 per cent an external locus of control.

Despite low scores on the stress and burnout scales, it was considered important to conduct regression analyses to determine which of the eight independent variables did help predict stress and burnout. It is vital to determine as many potential causes of stress and burnout as possible, not only to alleviate stress and burnout in individual sufferers, but also to prevent them occurring in other people. It is important to prevent the

* A full report of the method and results of this study can be found in Capel (1987).

unpleasant emotions and negative experiences building in individuals, which ultimately may be detrimental to pupils and the organization as well. Burned out individuals may show atypical behaviour patterns, e.g. may be short tempered or moan a lot, run out of imagination and/or enthusiasm, work long hours but not achieve anything, cannot relax or sleep, become mentally and emotionally exhausted, try to avoid contact with pupils and staff, may be absent a lot, or even leave the job or profession entirely. Only when specific sources of stress and burnout are identified can steps be taken to reduce their effect.

When looking at what variables were the best predictors of stress, burnout, and the components of burnout, results showed that locus of control was the best predictor of stress and personal accomplishment. An external locus of control was associated with higher stress and lower personal accomplishment. Role ambiguity was the best predictor of total burnout, of how frequently burnout was experienced and of depersonalization. Higher role ambiguity was associated with higher total burnout, experiencing burnout more frequently and depersonalizing pupils more. The total number of years' teaching experience was the best predictor of how strongly burnout was experienced, and the fewer the number of years' teaching experience was associated with experiencing burnout more strongly. The number of years in present position was the best predictor of emotional exhaustion. Fewer years in present position was associated with experiencing higher emotional exhaustion.

Locus of control, role conflict, role ambiguity, total number of years' teaching experience, number of years in present position and number of times school work was taken home to do each week, taken together, contributed toward an explanation of stress, total burnout, and all the subscales of burnout. Specifically, results showed that an external locus of control, higher role conflict, higher role ambiguity, fewer years as a teacher, fewer years in present position and taking school work home more frequently were associated with higher levels of stress and burnout, experiencing burnout more frequently and more strongly, higher levels of emotional exhaustion and depersonalization, and lower levels of personal accomplishment. The number of hours involved with extra-curricular activities and the number of different classes taught did not help explain stress and burnout in this study.

Discussion

LEVELS OF STRESS AND BURNOUT

This study looked at levels of stress and burnout among 78 teachers and then determined whether eight selected variables were related to stress and burnout in these teachers. None of the teachers reported experiencing high levels of stress and burnout, which contrasts with the 25 per cent generally reported in other studies. The reasons for this could be that teachers with high levels of stress and burnout have already left the profession, or did not return the questionnaire. This could be especially true for teachers with an external locus of control, because they do not see any point in returning the questionnaire, e.g. 'it will not make any difference if I return the questionnaire or not'. People with an external locus of control are likely to be those experiencing higher levels of stress and burnout and, therefore, this may be represented in the low levels of stress and burnout being reported by subjects in this study.

It could also be that because the study was conducted in the autumn term teachers had not yet built up high levels of stress and burnout. Maybe the 19 and 49 per cent of teachers experiencing medium levels of stress and burnout would report high levels of stress and burnout later in the school year.

Further, the small number of schools in the sample could have caused a bias toward low stress and burnout. The schools may have experienced low role conflict and role ambiguity because of their administrative structure (as seems likely, because the scores reported for role conflict and role ambiguity were low). Including other schools may reduce this bias and get a truly representative sample of the amounts and causes of stress in teachers from many different schools, with many different administrative structures.

CAUSES OF STRESS AND BURNOUT

Despite low levels of stress and burnout, the results confirm that burnout, like stress, is a complex issue, with a combination of causal factors determining a person's likelihood of suffering burnout. Whatever the levels of stress and burnout, they may negatively affect the individual (e.g. mental and emotional exhaustion, a lower sense of personal accomplishment), the pupils (e.g. the burned-out teacher gives them less information, less praise, and pays less attention to individuals and their needs), and the organization (e.g. higher absenteeism, working hard but not accomplishing anything, leaving the job or the profession entirely). Steps must therefore be taken to combat the problem. In this study, six factors were found to contribute toward the prediction of stress and burnout in teachers. Steps should be taken to eliminate the negative effects of these factors, as well as remove the factors from the environment as far as possible.

IMPLICATIONS FOR INDIVIDUAL TEACHERS

Individual teachers should assess each of the factors identified in this study, plus others which have been identified in other studies, or which may seem important factors in producing stress and burnout for them, to determine how they relate to stress and burnout for them personally. Individual teachers are responsible for identifying factors which are potential stressors for them, reducing or eliminating risks, taking steps to avoid stressful situations, and reducing stress when it occurs by developing a wide range of stress-reducing mechanisms. They need training in conflict resolution skills, as well as knowledge of many stress-reducing mechanisms they can employ to counteract the stress, e.g. removing themselves temporarily from the stressful situation and focusing on another aspect of the job, having a complete change of activity, such as taking exercise or reading a book, or using relaxation techniques. They can then determine which are effective for them individually.

Role conflict can be reduced by each teacher having a clear job description, developed jointly by the teacher and headteacher, specific to the individual situation. Teachers need to be involved in developing realistic individual and organizational short- and long-term goals and objectives. They need to know who they are directly responsible to, and have effective channels of communication with all those with whom they work. The messages coming from the headteacher, other teachers and parents must be compatible, otherwise there will be conflict between the demands from all these people. Teachers can reduce role ambiguity by knowing exactly how they are being evaluated on the job, how to perform adequately, and how they can advance in the job.

Teachers with an internal locus of control experienced less burnout than teachers with an external locus of control. Central government and local education authority administrators and headteachers should recognize this and include teachers in democratic decision making on matters which are of direct concern and importance to them. These may be administrative or organizational decisions (e.g. the individual time-table), or professional decisions related directly to teaching (e.g. implementing new initiatives such as GCSE or TVEI, having a say on conditions of service and on personal job description, and what is needed on 'Baker Days'). At the present time there are so many reforms at all levels being introduced into schools that many teachers feel they have little or no control over their own actions. This may be increasing the amount of stress and burnout being experienced by teachers throughout the country.

Further, teachers need to take work home less frequently during the week. They can then get a complete break from the job, and come back refreshed and ready to start again the next day.

IMPLICATIONS FOR HEADTEACHERS

Headteachers should develop strategies to prevent staff stress and burn-out through staff development activities, and the general organization and management of the school, e.g. making sure staff have the necessary tools to implement new initiatives, consulting with staff on changes taking place in the school. They must also help identify burned-out teachers and take steps to reduce burnout in that individual, e.g. a supportive atmosphere is one essential feature of schools that are less stressful or in which teachers are helped to overcome or eliminate burnout more successfully.

IMPLICATIONS FOR CENTRAL GOVERNMENT AND LOCAL EDUCATION AUTHORITIES

Central government and local education authority administrators have a vital role to play in reducing or eliminating stress and burnout among teachers. They must acknowledge that burned-out teachers are going through a negative experience, and are not 100 per cent effective in their jobs. This is not only detrimental to them, but also to the children, school and other staff. Further, burned-out teachers may leave the school or the profession entirely.

Central government and local education authorities should therefore be familiar with the antecedents of stress and burnout among teachers in general. Steps should be taken at both national and local levels to reduce the antecedents of stress and burnout in the teaching profession in general, e.g. reducing the amount of change occurring in the profession at any one time, so that teachers have time to adjust to new initiatives before something else is thrust upon them; reducing uncertainty, e.g. planned school closures or mergers; and recognizing the good work that teachers do. Central government and local education authorities may undertake research on the stressful effects of change itself and of particular policies they implement. By doing this, they may become more aware of the impact of constant change on the teachers and be able to reduce the stressful effects of this change. Further, local education authorities may introduce in-service courses on stress management, which may help reduce stress and burnout among teachers and help them cope with this (see Hall *et al.*, this volume, for more information).

IMPLICATIONS FOR PERSONS INVOLVED WITH THE TRAINING OF TEACHERS

Persons involved with initial and in-service courses of teacher training also have an important role to play in reducing or eliminating stress and burnout. They must recognize the problems and causes of stress and burnout among teachers, then help prepare teachers for problems they are likely to face, and possible ways of solving these problems, e.g. giving role-playing exercises, such as those given on stress inoculation training in the chapter by Esteve. They must also help teachers recognize factors which contribute to stress and burnout in them personally and provide them with several stress-reducing mechanisms from which they can choose.

OTHER VARIABLES WHICH MAY BE IMPORTANT IN PREDICTING STRESS AND BURNOUT

Although these six factors of higher role conflict, higher role ambiguity, an external locus of control, fewer years in the teaching profession, fewer years in present position and taking work home did contribute more frequently to stress and burnout among the teachers in this sample, they predicted less than 40 per cent of stress and burnout. However, this amount of variance is high compared to other studies, e.g. Capel (1986) accounted for 24 per cent, at most, of variance in burnout in athletic trainers, and Schwab (1981) accounted for 24 per cent, at most, of variance in teachers. However, this result does imply that other variables must help predict the remaining 60 per cent of variance.

Other studies, therefore, need to be conducted to determine what other factors help predict stress and burnout among teachers. These factors may include individual variables (e.g. personality, level of commitment to teaching), or organizational variables (e.g. administrative structure, school climate). Any studies conducted to determine other important variables must, however, include both individual and organizational factors, as research has shown that it is an interaction between these two which is the important factor in explaining stress and burnout. A further study is currently being conducted by the author to determine whether stress and burnout levels increase during the school year, and what other factors may contribute to stress and burnout among teachers.

The problems of stress and burnout, therefore, need to be tackled from as many different fronts as possible. The problem can only be tackled effectively by cooperation at every level. Through recognition of the problem at all levels steps may be taken to reduce and eliminate the devastating experiences of stress and burnout. Unique solutions to the unique causes and manifestations of stress and burnout in any one teacher can then be dealt with effectively. Likewise, the incidence of stress and burnout in other teachers can be reduced or eliminated.

References

Begley, D. (1982). Burnout among special education administrators. Paper presented at the Annual Convention of the Council for Exceptional Children, Houston, Texas.

Blase, J. (1982). A social–psychological grounded theory of teacher stress and burnout. *Educational Administration Quarterly* **18**(4), 93–113.

Capel, S. A. (1986). Psychological and organizational factors related to burnout in athletic trainers. *Research Quarterly for Exercise and Sport* **57**(4), 321–8.

Capel, S. A. (1987). The incidence of and influences on stress and burnout in secondary school teachers. *British Journal of Educational Psychology* **57**(3), 279–88.

Capel, S. A., Sisley, B. L. and Desertrain, G. S. (1987). The relationship of role conflict and role ambiguity to burnout in high school basketball coaches. *Journal of Sport Psychology* **9**(2), 106–17.

Cooley, E. and Savicki, V. (1981). Preliminary investigations of environmental and individual aspects of burnout in teachers. Paper presented at Oregon Education Association, Otter Rock, Oregon.

Daley, M. R. (1979). Burnout: Smouldering problem in protective services. *Social Work* **24**(5), 375–9.

Dunham, J. (1976). Stress situations and responses. In National Association of Schoolmasters (ed.), *Stress in Schools*. National Association of Schoolmasters: Hemel Hempstead, Herts.

Fielding, M. (1982). Personality and situational correlates of teacher stress and burnout. Doctoral Dissertation, University of Oregon. *Dissertation Abstracts International*, 43/02A.

Freudenberger, H. J. (1974). Staff burn-out. *Journal of Social Issues* **30**(1), 159–65.

Kahn, R., Wolfe, D., Quinn, D., Snoek, R. and Rosenthal, J. (1964). *Organizational Stress: Studies in Role Conflict and Role Ambiguity*. John Wiley: New York.

Kyriacou, C. and Sutcliffe, J. (1978a). Teacher stress: Prevalence, sources and symptoms. *British Journal of Educational Psychology* **48**, 159–67.

Kyriacou, C. and Sutcliffe, J. (1978b). Teacher stress and satisfaction. *Educational Research* **21**(2), 89–96.

Lawrenson, G. and McKinnon, A. (1982). A survey of classroom teachers of the emotionally disturbed: Attrition and burnout factors. *Behavioral Disorders* **8**(1), 41–8.

Mancini, V., Wuest, D., Clark, E. and Ridosh, N. (1982). A comparison of the interaction patterns and academic learning time of low-burnout and high-burnout physical educators. Paper presented at the Big Ten Symposium on Research on Teaching, Lafayette, Indiana.

Mancini, V., Wuest, D., Vantine, K. and Clark, E. (1984). The use of instruction and supervision in interaction analysis on burned out teachers: Its effects on teaching behaviors, level of burnout, and academic learning time. *Journal of Teaching in Physical Education* **3**(2), 29–46.

Martens, R. (1982). *Sport Competition Anxiety Test*. Human Kinetics Publishers: Champaign, Illinois.

Maslach, C. and Jackson, S. (1981). *Maslach Burnout Inventory*. Consulting Psychologists Press: Palo Alto, California.

Nagy, S. (1982). The relationship of type A personalities, workaholism, perceptions of the school climate, and years of teaching experience to burnout of
  elementary and junior high school teachers in northwest Oregon school
  district. Unpublished doctoral dissertation, University of Oregon, Eugene,
  Oregon.
Pines, A. (1982a). Helpers motivation and the burnout syndrome. In Wills, T. A.
  (ed.), *Basic Processes in Helping Relationships*. Academic Press: London and San
  Diego.
Pines, A. (1982b). Changing organizations. Is a work environment without
  burnout an impossible goal? In Paine, W. S. (ed.), *Job Stress and Burnout*,
  pp. 189–211. Sage Publications: Beverly Hills, California.
Pines, A. and Aronson, E. (1981). *Burnout: From Tedium to Personal Growth*. Free
  Press: New York.
Rizzo, J., House, R. and Lirtzman, S. (1970). Role conflict and role ambiguity in
  complex organizations. *Administrative Science Quarterly* **15**, 150–63.
Rotter, J. B. (1966). Generalized expectancies for internal versus external control
  of reinforcement. *Psychological Monographs*, **80**(1), monograph no. 609.
Schwab, R. L. (1981). The relationship of role conflict, role ambiguity, teacher
  background variables and perceived burnout among teachers. Doctoral
  Dissertation, University of Connecticut. *Dissertation Abstracts International*,
  41(09-A)2, 3823-a.
Westerhouse, M. A. (1979). The effects of tenure, role conflict and role conflict
  resolution on the work orientation and burnout of teachers. Doctoral Dissertation, University of California at Berkeley. *Dissertation Abstracts International*,
  41(01A), 8014928, 174.
Zabel, R. and Zabel, M. K. (1982). Factors in burnout among teachers of
  exceptional children. *Exceptional Children* **49**, 261–3.

COPING AND SEN: CHALLENGING IDEALISM

Andrea Freeman

This paper considers the relationships between three complex areas:
teacher coping, special educational needs and teacher education. The
underlying theme is that idealism is developed in teachers through their
professional education, but the reality of the school begins to corrode it
through social pressures and the challenge of their contacts in the
classroom with pupils with special educational needs. Some empirical
evidence is offered which was obtained from a sample of teachers from
a large comprehensive school, and a sample of teachers attending full-
time in-service courses in special educational needs, in support of the
contention.

The development of idealism

Initial courses for teacher education are a powerful resocialization process, where the novitiate is introduced to the culture of schools and schooling and the profession of teaching with its skills, principles, values and professional pride.

Harris (1982) also considers teachers to be in an invidious position in that they are given the task of transmitting what is worthwhile from the culture to the pupils, including personal and social development, but at the same time work within institutions which are designed to exercise social control through the reproduction of the social order. This clearly illustrates the complexity of the relationship between the teacher, the school, social institutions and the economic climate.

To some extent this is founded in the notions relating to ideal teachers, which are generated in society generally and within the institutions where the teacher education takes place. An example of society's views of ideal teachers is that they should be paragons of virtue and set an example to children, and that they should know almost everything (children certainly tell their parents this). Certain personality characteristics are also expected, and if the teacher teaches children with any obvious special needs this expectation is amplified – patience is the quality which is considered vital rather than dynamism or teaching skills (e.g. Simpson, 1972). The general public appears to consider that the good teacher is the one who can control the children and make them learn, regardless of the content of the learning or of the methods used, within reason.

The rhetoric within the institutions about ideal teachers is equally strong, so that students endeavour to build a personal reality from a model presented via their professional studies, to develop a shared meaning of what it is to be a teacher. Within any community people develop understandings which can be described as shared meanings. These enable people to pursue similar goals and to work harmoniously together. Learning to be a teacher involves learning the role – learning the social construction of teaching. Part of the socialization of the student teacher involves the development of professional idealism which is immediately recognizable by cynical old hands in teaching, and which involves notions about the expertise within the profession, self-confidence and a number of precepts again related to ideas about the good teacher. Good teachers, for example, take account of individual differences within a class; good teachers do not have discipline problems; good teachers perform consistently well; good teachers are well prepared; good teachers like all children in the class; and so on.

In order to become a good teacher, students are introduced to a number of rituals and processes which will arm them magically against problems that they may encounter in the classroom. And on teaching practice they are supported by tutors who can re-emphasize the rituals even though things do not appear to be going well. But, of course, tutor behaviour is influenced by their understandings of ideal students, ideal teachers and the idealized tasks that the students are to undertake. Rituals are often not recognized as such, since they form a commonplace experience for everyone. They are very powerful in exerting social control, and this may happen very rapidly. For example, in an analysis of milk-time in a class of reception pupils, the ritual of distributing straws and milk had a very controlling effect within 4 days (Dodgson, 1987). Rituals have the advantage of enabling us to operate efficiently, and in this way are similar to stereotyping. Greetings are an obvious example. If we did not receive the reply 'Very well' to our greeting we would be surprised and probably unpleasantly disconcerted. This is even experienced by general practitioners when enquiring after a patient's health – so strong is the ritualized response. Rituals are also part of the transmission of culture, and clearly form part of a group's culture.

In schools there are many rituals, such as calling a register, and in primary schools it can be argued that the establishment of clear rituals, in addition to ensuring social control, also enables pupils to concentrate on other aspects of learning, by reducing the degree of uncertainty, increasing confidence and enabling them to focus their attention on the task in hand. For children with special educational needs, students learning the rituals of the classroom and school are introduced to another array of processes and procedures which form their armoury to enable them to 'help' the children with special needs and at the same time to cope. The rhetoric of special educational needs gives the impression of neatly sequential procedures, with uncomplicated interprofessional cooperation, happy parental participation and available support. There is also an implicit assumption that it is for the benefit of the child (see Apple, 1979; Edelman, 1977; Freeman, 1988). The reality is quite different: procedures are not tidily applied, professionals squabble in power struggles and vested interests, parents are thought to be interfering nuisances, and support is not available on request. The rituals and procedures do not protect the beginning teacher, as other more powerful magic is at work. The description by Lortie (1975) of teachers' views of their professional training is perhaps relevant here, and a sentiment also expressed by British teachers, in that most teachers considered that they had learnt how to teach while working, and dismissed their college or university training as irrelevant.

My interpretation of this is that idealism is challenged once 'real' work begins. The rituals to protect oneself on teaching practice may not work, but the tutor is there to reassure. Once employed, other social realities take over, including:

1 Hierarchical systems within the school, e.g. the head may not wish his/her staff to talk to visiting professionals.
2 Allocation of resources, according to criteria understood only by long-established members of staff.
3 Setting of priorities, which may conflict with the new teacher's priorities, e.g. emphasizing high achievement rather than whole school approaches.
4 Favouritism, cliques and social groupings, which can act as powerful pressure groups influencing policy and practice within the school.
5 Traditions and the associated perspectives and theories, which serve as explanations for current practices, and appear to require no further justification, even though the new teacher may find the practices old-fashioned or ethically unacceptable.
6 School recipes for action, the way that things have always been done and done 'successfully'.

All of these involve other forms of rituals and procedures idiosyncratic to the social setting of the particular school and forming a different selection of shared meanings. In some schools, some of the shared meanings are contradictory and operate against each other, creating problems of development. An example of this was discovered in a school which asked for an evaluation of its special needs provision. There were a number of conflicting understandings of special needs within the school, which was confusing the teachers and pupils about the aims of education there.

It will be argued in greater detail later that children with special educational needs are particularly challenging to teachers in two ways. First, those teachers who make a positive choice to be special needs teachers may be more idealistic than others in that they feel that schooling fails some children, and they wish to improve the lot of the child with special needs. Secondly, pupils challenge teachers' feelings of professional competence and confidence through providing examples of mismatch between what the teacher expects and what happens in the classroom. Children with special needs can challenge teaching styles, understandings of how learning occurs, classroom processes, group management, task analysis, the ideals of education, and personal reactions to pupils.

A dilemma for teachers is the divide between their professional idealism and the reality of the classroom, where they can become frustrated and unable to use their expertise. Woods (1979) has argued that teachers use a range of strategies for survival which often look as if they are 'teaching', and which (usually) can be educationally justified, at least in the short term. He identified seven coping strategies:

- domination: 'to alarm and to rally, but the aim is singlefold – conformity' (p. 153);

- negotiation: in which the teacher exchanges good behaviour of the class with release from 'work';
- fraternization: being one of them and allowing more liberty;
- absence or removal of self or of individual pupils;
- ritual and routine;
- occupational therapy: engaging in activities which pupils are thought to enjoy and which require little thought or effort;
- morale boosting: a shared identification of the pupils as the common enemy to be belittled in the staffroom.

Pollard (1980) also argues that the ideal pedagogical practices which teachers have identified as part of their professionalism are modified in the light of five self-interests which come between the teacher and his/her idealism in order to cope with the reality of the job. He suggests that these five self-interests are:

- self-image: maintaining a professional self-image while adapting to pragmatic considerations;
- work load: getting through the week by conserving energy;
- health and stress: coping with fatigue and stress by modifying teaching practices;
- enjoyment: avoiding boredom, maintaining interest and being liked by pupils;
- autonomy: the protection of personal independence and autonomy.

These approaches to understanding the way that idealism is modified in real situations, through their conceptualization of the modifications to idealism that teachers make as coping strategies, are sufficient at a general level, but in order to explain the modifications which an individual might make requires a psychological explanation. A major problem in all stress and coping research is being able to explain individual differences, and individual variability. One attempt to explain individual differences and variability is described below.

A model of coping

A model of stress and coping was developed as a result of research into teacher stress and coping (see Freeman, 1986). The conceptual framework of the model is based upon an hierarchical model of the cognitive system and certain theoretical understandings of stress and coping. Stress is defined in this model as an awareness of not coping, which is considered to be in part an ongoing normal process. This is in line with Haan's (1977) position who considers that coping is the 'normative mode'. This process is perceived by oneself and others as personal, in the sense that it is oneself that must cope, and additionally in terms of having a personal style. It also involves complex cognitive skills, since there is a great deal of information which must be processed, in order to respond appropriately. This applies particularly to interruptions to ongoing behaviours, when there is a risk of emotional upset and confusion from too much information.

The major innovation in this model lies in its explanatory power through the use of the cognitive model which suggests that there are two distinct forms of coping which are qualitatively different. The model describes everyday ongoing coping on which we are unable to introspect, and the problem-solving level of coping which is accessible to consciousness. These are based upon Morris (1981). He put forward a cognitive model describing the two levels as BOSS and EMPLOYEE. The characteristics of BOSS functions are:

- they are executive functions, and monitor EMPLOYEE functions;
- they are conscious;
- they are intentional;
- they are flexible;
- they are of limited capacity: that is each individual has a fixed capacity for BOSS functions beyond which they experience overload.

On the other hand, EMPLOYEE functions can be described as:

- they are non-intentional;
- they are not conscious and therefore not open to introspection;
- they are of unlimited capacity;
- they control low-level specific activities required to fulfil a BOSS command;
- they convert incoming information into formats 'used by the cognitive system (e.g. words, semantics, the objects of visual perception)' (Morris, 1981, p. 195);
- they include all the cognitive systems involved in perceiving, remembering, performing actions, etc.;
- they use the 'incoming information to act upon the environment in fairly stereotyped ways which do not require BOSS for their direction' (Morris, 1981, p. 195).

The difference between the two can be described using a driving analogy. Many of us drive home or along another familiar route, and wonder how we arrived at our destination, as we had not been conscious of our actions, but thinking about something else, in other words operating at an automatic pilot level as far as our driving was concerned.

However, if a dog had run into the road we would immediately have become fully aware, since the novelty and unexpectedness of the event would have ensured that BOSS, or problem-solving functions would become involved. Figure 3.1 summarizes the model.

Coping can therefore be described as an ongoing process at EMPLOYEE level or automatic pilot. This process is monitored by BOSS until a potentially stressful event occurs, at which point BOSS will intervene through the appraisal process (as long as BOSS is not overloaded, in which case BOSS will be unable to even be aware). If the event is a false alarm, then coping will continue at EMPLOYEE level. If the situation is appraised as potentially threatening, then BOSS will take over to try to solve the problem(s) and conscious intentional strategies will be employed, e.g. seeking help from a friend, deciding to talk to the person concerned in a particular way, deliberately using relaxation techniques, using positive thinking. Once the coping strategies have been employed and are relatively successful, then BOSS will attend to other matters, allowing EMPLOYEE to continue.

This two-level model of coping can also help us to understand why the same event may make us feel stressed on one occasion but not on another, in that changes occur over time and the demands on BOSS vary. For example, in a classroom, the teacher may feel confident in his/her approach, may enjoy teaching the class and find it challenging, may know that there is a supportive colleague in the next room, may feel happy

---

A. Automatic pilot
- overlearned strategies (from childhood)
- unplanned
- often inappropriate in extreme circumstances

Position of
threshold
depends on   --
personal state
resources and
stressors,
i.e. appraisal

B. Conscious coping strategies, e.g. problem solving
- planned
- preoccupying
- limited capacity
- intentional

Fig. 3.1   BOSS and EMPLOYEE thresholds.

about his/her domestic situation, and feel rested and generally healthy. If a potentially stressful situation arises, the teacher will be better able to cope than if he/she had been awake all night, or the colleague in the next room were unsupportive, or he/she did not enjoy teaching that class, or were concerned about a problem at home, or felt off-colour. Teaching in itself will engage BOSS attention, since it requires flexibility and attention to novel events – in other words thinking on one's feet – regardless of the additional attention required to ensure the smooth running of the classroom. Most teachers have experienced either personally or vicariously a sudden apparently inexplicable loss of temper over a trivial matter to the shock of the pupils concerned. This is where there is an overload at BOSS level and the coping strategies employed, instead of being conscious and controlled by BOSS, are probably those learned in childhood which are part of the EMPLOYEE repertoire. The strategies used by EMPLOYEE coping functions are those which have been overlearned, and can be used more or less automatically, which is why many adult coping strategies are fundamentally childish ones that are slightly modified – sulking, tantrums, storming off, running away, refusing food, being destructive. Table 3.2 shows these aspects for different car driving situations, showing how the two forms of coping interact.*

Table 3.2 BOSS and EMPLOYEE coping functions.

Situation	Coping level		Effectiveness
	BOSS	*EMPLOYEE*	
Learner driver	High engagement -overload	Lack of overlearned strategies that appropriate	Feelings of anxiety, stressed
Experienced driver in routine situation	Low engagement	Strategies overlearned	Efficient, copes well
Experienced driver in adverse weather	High engagement	Overlearned strategies appropriate	Efficient, copes well, enjoys the challenge
Experienced driver in extremely adverse weather	High engagement -overload	Some overlearned strategies inappropriate	Stressed, feelings of panic

* My thanks to the editors for this example.

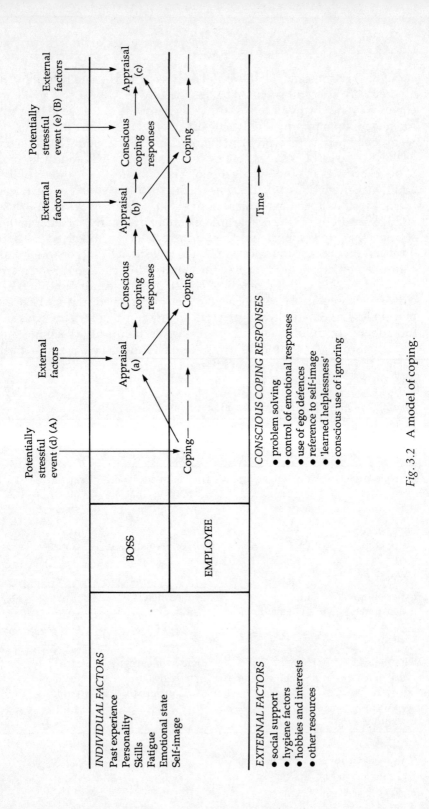

Fig. 3.2 A model of coping.

Between the two levels of coping is a threshold, which is also a decision point for whether BOSS will be involved in the coping process or not, since EMPLOYEE coping is continuous. The level of the threshold will vary according to both personal state, and other factors within the environment, including health, social support, perceived personal competence, self-esteem, etc. Identification of oneself as stressed occurs at the BOSS level through appraisal, once the EMPLOYEE coping strategies have been found inappropriate (such as laughing at the wrong time) or insufficient (feeling at a loss to know what to do). If the threshold is low then the individual will experience stress more often, since he/she will be conscious of a lack of coping (see Freeman, in press, for a fuller discussion). Thus the best copers rarely experience stress, since they cope with the bulk of potential stressors at the EMPLOYEE level (see Fig. 3.2).

For teachers the threshold is very important, because teaching is thinking and problem-solving almost continuously. This will take up much of BOSS's limited capacity, which means that if the teacher is experiencing stress he/she will inevitably be using BOSS for coping. Thus the teaching strategies used may become more rigid, less creative, and less relevant to the pupils than when the teacher is feeling unstressed. The way that teachers appraise their situation is, therefore, crucial to the self-definition of stress, and to the difference in the threshold level. If, for example, the teacher defines him/herself as being an incompetent person, this is likely to give rise to stress through the lowering of the threshold to give him/her more awareness of potentially stressful occurrences.

Three aspects appear to be important in contributing to the appraisal process: *autonomy*, *competence* and *satisfaction*. The teacher's autonomy in the classroom is traditional, and involves responsibility for everything that takes place there. Teachers define their own roles, as do most workers. Even if they have job descriptions which delineate clearly their duties, different people will make the job their own. Where there are a number of similar posts within a school, e.g. year tutors, each post-holder operates quite differently, to the annoyance of other staff. Part of the role definition is the legitimation of tasks. If teachers are asked to undertake tasks which they consider to be a legitimate part of their job, even if they feel tired, they are unlikely to feel stressed. Stress arises from demands which are viewed as unreasonable or not a legitimate aspect of the role, either through perceptions of their own lack of skills or through an unreasonable imposition by incompetent colleagues. The teacher feels responsible even if the class is known to be particularly difficult when they come from a certain teacher. This is partly due to the tacit understanding of teaching as a performing art, where the teacher is performing for the audience of pupils. This is very risky because performance varies depending on mood, attitudes, previous experience, physical health, etc., and again on the level of the threshold between the two levels of coping for that lesson. In addition, there is no guarantee that what worked once will work again. Teachers often speak of their job as if they were performing, playing a part, pretending to be cross, and cherish those times when the class was thoroughly involved and absorbed and eating out of their hands.

These aspects are related to competence. Schools are highly competitive places for teachers as well as pupils. Teachers who are perceived as failures or stressed (and often the two are equated quite wrongly) may be avoided by the more successful teachers as though the condition were contagious. This usually leads to a faster decline due to the lack of social support, but signals the success of the survivors. In this situation the teacher is more likely to be using BOSS capacity to cope on an almost continual basis, which means that his/her teaching will probably become less relevant for the pupils and create more problems through rigidity and boredom. The threshold will be lowered to the extent that the teacher is also almost continually aware of not coping, which in turn leads to self-definitions of incompetence and loss of confidence into a vicious circle of decline. Competence is closely related to performance. If the performance does not go well, then the teacher takes personal responsibility. Problems arise when the teacher is unable to perform well due to feeling unwell – this may not matter for a short period and pupils are often very well behaved for the teacher who loses his/her voice, but if it is a prolonged sub-clinical condition, then tolerance of the pupils may be lost, since pupils are not very forgiving of teachers who do not perform well. This is the time when colleagues may notice a rise in the noise level from the classroom and start to think of that teacher as incompetent. It is interesting that those aspects which make teachers feel inadequate are the same as the ones which they use to identify their colleagues as incompetent. Noise levels in classrooms is an example of this, as are poor organization and time management.

The third aspect is job satisfaction. Most teachers have identified their desire to work with people as the motivation to become teachers. One of the strongest themes in the literature on teaching is that teachers get their satisfaction from the positive relationships and feedback which they obtain from pupils, not only from their teaching activities but also from the pastoral and moral welfare aspects of the job (Freeman, 1987). Thus, for example, Payne (1974) found that teachers in EPA schools consider their jobs more satisfying than other teaching jobs. Positive feedback loops take time to become established, as supply teachers, probationers and those new to the job can testify. Pupils can be unforgiving if they consider that the teacher has not behaved competently, and may withdraw their goodwill for a time, perhaps for the rest of the school year. This is only likely to happen in extreme cases, but is most likely to happen to teachers who mishandle a disruptive pupil. But even a minor interruption to a lesson can break the feedback loop, and require hard work from the teacher to regain the previous position. Job satisfaction is very important as it has an inverse relationship with stress, i.e. the more a teacher is satisfied in his/her job the less likely he/she is to experience stress. Additionally, the satisfied teacher probably feels more professional esteem and, therefore, probably performs better. This also means that BOSS can concentrate more on the pedagogical aspects of work and coping can continue at the EMPLOYEE level.

It is not surprising that teachers experience greater stress from special needs pupils, since the challenge that they make to the teachers' idealism, rituals and procedures will be greater. If the adage that if you want to find a fault in a system put a child in it is true, then putting a child with special needs into a school system can have a similarly revealing effect. All three aspects delineated above will be challenged by special needs pupils. Many teachers define special needs as outside their role, and certainly not included in legitimated tasks (typified by statements beginning 'It's not my job to . . .'). This is reinforced by statements to indicate feelings of inadequacy and incompetence ('I haven't been trained to . . .'). Finally, teachers take into account the effects it may have on their positive feedback loops from the class; if the pupil requires more attention and time than other pupils the loops may be threatened. Or, if the teacher does not pay enough attention to the pupil and the others feel it is unjust there could be problems.

Rituals which usually work with a class may not work with special needs pupils. For example, setting a test may give the teacher a breathing space and pupils appear to quite like this sort of activity, but for the special needs pupil the tactic may create more problems for the teacher because:

- the pupil cannot read the questions;
- the pupil cannot do the work;
- the pupil does not concentrate;
- the pupil does not accept this form of oppression;
- the pupil may see the situation as a good opportunity for disruption;
- the pupil may be emotionally distressed, etc.

or, to summarize, the teacher has misjudged the situation.

Students on teaching practice may also feel challenged by the special needs pupils, especially in their desire to be good teachers, provide appropriate work for all pupils, and maintain classroom control. In their case this challenge is made more piquant by the anxiety that they may fail their teaching practice. Dodgson (1987) has developed a model of how problems arise for teachers based on two ideal aspects of the 'good teacher' – control and preparation. The ritualized preparation of lesson plans and the rigid control of all pupils in the classroom all of the time are assumed to enable the teacher magically to cope and *the pupils to learn*. Since these forms of magic do neither, the teacher is in a quandary, and feels that more preparation or more control is necessary. When these fail, outside agencies are approached to provide their forms of magic through different rituals. These agencies may tacitly support the teacher's idea that she is incompetent, by making suggestions about planning and control (these are the usual strategies of educational psychologists and support teachers). As these two aspects are in themselves sources of stress, the teacher finds herself in a cycle of self-definition of inadequacy and incompetence, with the only other alternatives to blame the pupils, or to blame the other agencies as useless (Dodgson, 1987).

Idealism and reality

An evaluation of the special educational needs provision in a comprehensive school was undertaken, and a complex picture built up from a variety of sources which enabled triangulation of the data. Briefly, the underpinning problem appeared to be the confusion in the definition of special education needs within the school, in spite of a well-written school policy document. This confusion was evident in information from both the teachers and the pupils. It affected the way that the teachers individually defined their roles in relationship to the special needs pupils, and their feelings of competence and responsibility to them. In addition, this influenced their definitions of resources required, including other professionals and 'experts'. The major pressure was from their perceived lack of time to undertake the many tasks required of them, and this in turn led to doubts about their own competence, and was seen by teachers and pupils alike to affect positive social relationships between the pupils and teachers. The staff appeared to be confident in their own teaching ability and considered their colleagues to be competent and the school management satisfactory. However, the fundamental underlying problem for the school appears to be the lack of a clear philosophy about the aims of the school which would enable them to include the special needs pupils within the community.

As part of this evaluation, a questionnaire was devised which sought to obtain information about stress and special educational needs. This questionnaire was also given to teachers attending full-time in-service (INSET) courses in special needs. It covered the following:

- job satisfaction,
- social support,
- locus of control,
- factors to relieve pressure,

- priority concerns,
- role factors,
- contact with special needs pupils,
- attitudes towards special needs pupils,
- bothersome and frequent problems.

These aspects were chosen due to their prominence in the research literature on teacher stress (Stensrud and Stensrud, 1983; Cruichshank *et al.*, 1974; Dunham, 1984; Fletcher and Payne, 1982; Kyriacou and Sutcliffe, 1979; Pettegrew and Wolf, 1982).

The findings have been summarized to identify similarities between the school-based study and the INSET group, and to draw out differences in their idealism and the way that the special educational needs pupils challenge them.

The first interesting differences and similarities in the two groups were found in a series of incomplete sentences which sought to identify the teachers' attitudes towards children with special educational needs. Both groups found children with special needs more rewarding to teach – perhaps because of the circumstances within which they operate. The school sample commented particularly on the personal characteristics of the children, both negative and positive, and this aspect was closely followed by the INSET group.

Although one of the themes that the INSET group was exposed to on the course was the lack of uniqueness of special needs pupils, remarkably few INSET teachers mentioned this. Their feelings about children with special needs were very similar, with professional concerns coming first, followed by personal ones. When asked about their biggest problem in teaching pupils with special needs, the groups differed. The school group showed the reality of their classroom life – they felt the lack of skills, were unsure how to modify the work they set, and time did not allow them to do what they consider necessary. The INSET group appeared to express the notion that they could solve all problems for the individual children if they had unlimited time, stressing an understanding of learning that is teacher-directed, and part of the old ethos of the remedial teacher. As far as the parents of children with special needs were concerned, the attitudes of both groups were similar and typical, expressing the two contradictory views that parents are unrealistic, unqualified and uncaring, or cooperative, caring and concerned. When completing the sentence 'Children with special educational needs often . . .', the two groups again showed remarkable differences, with the school group emphasizing equally their positive attributes, and their learning difficulties. The INSET group noted their learning difficulties and the discrimination against them, taking a pessimistic view. This would appear to be part of the INSET group's perception of their schools and the injustices that affect their pupils. It can be interpreted as a result of their idealism which has made them more aware of the injustices, compared to the school group who perhaps are more reality-based with lower expectations. Teaching materials were thought by the school group to be scarce, inappropriate and not available. The INSET group, on the other hand, considered teaching materials to be good and improving. For the teachers in both groups the major concern was with the adequacy of the schooling provided for children with special needs, the attitudes towards them, and the time available.

The second area where the similarities and differences between the two groups is highlighted is where they were asked to identify their most frequent and troublesome problems. This enables a separation to be made between those minor irritations which are frequent and have the effect of accumulating, leading to a wearing down, compared to a major but infrequent event. The effects of resocialization through the full-time INSET courses can be seen most clearly in their rankings on these items. For the most frequent problems the school group felt stressed and anxious and could not get enough time to improve their pupils' achievement, including the special needs pupils. These problems are classroom orientated and appear to be reality orientated and practical, indicating a concern for self-survival perhaps. In contrast, the INSET group found aspects outside of their control and outside of their ordinary working routine the most frequent problems (e.g. wanting to change conditions out of school to improve pupils' lives, wanting to change parents' attitudes about themselves, etc.). These are far more idealistic and impractical – wanting change in the social conditions and in others, particularly where teachers are more or less powerless, typifies these problems.

The picture is similar for the most bothersome problems, in that it is again the school group who were experiencing stress and time pressures, while being concerned with pupil learning, in addition to wanting parents and pupils to have positive attitudes towards themselves. The INSET group also found bothersome wanting positive attitudes but they also wanted changes in the social conditions out of school to improve pupils' lives. The only classroom-orientated task which is highly ranked as bothersome is 'accomplishing tasks considered essential for pupil learning' (ranked fifth equal), which is perhaps a time pressure. For the combined rankings of frequent and bothersome problems the picture is similar, showing the school group to be far more classroom orientated compared to the outward looking and more idealistic INSET group. The school group are dominated by their own stress and anxiety, with time pressures in getting tasks completed adding to the stress. They were frequently bothered by their concern to motivate and enable pupils, including those with special educational needs, to learn and have positive attitudes towards education. The INSET group, on the other hand, found attitudes towards schooling, and attitudes of parents and pupils towards themselves, together with the social contexts within which they work, most frequently bothersome. It is interesting to note that ranked 6.6= is wanting the skills necessary to enable children to learn. This would imply a feeling of incompetence. But compared to the school group, the INSET teachers' horizons are far from the classroom.

The results show that approximately 30 per cent of all of the teachers were not satisfied with teaching as a profession, and this mirrors the usual figures of approximately 30 per cent of teachers who report that they are experiencing considerable stress at work. However, few were not satisfied with their performance as teachers (4 per cent of the school group and 0 per cent of the INSET group).

The greatest differences between the two groups occurred in the areas of syllabus, organization and management, where the school sample were considerably more satisfied than the special needs INSET students. The status of teachers in the area of special needs is probably reflected here, and the low priority that some schools accord their special needs provision.

Another aspect of job satisfaction is the ability to complete tasks, i.e. to have enough time to do what is self-defined as necessary professional tasks. Time pressures were highlighted for both groups in various questions; 'more time' ranked fourth in the list of factors to reduce pressure for both groups. A total of 86 per cent of both groups reported that they did not have enough time in question 6 (on overload). For the school group this was emphasized in the section on frequent and bothersome problems. The most frequent problem was 'getting time to accomplish personal goals' with 'completing professional goals' ranked fifth. They ranked second and fifth equal for bothersomeness. For the INSET group, two of the problems which involve time pressures were highly ranked – 'getting time to accomplish personal goals' ranked 1.5= for frequent problems and 'accomplish tasks considered essential for pupil learning' ranked fifth equal for bothersome problems.

The confidence of teachers is also important, and may be closely linked to teacher performance. For the teachers in the school, one of their frequent and bothersome problems was in 'feeling confident in teaching pupils with special educational needs', which was not included in the INSET group's list. They did, however, appear to lack confidence in their own skills 'to enable children to learn'. However, in contrast, 45 per cent of the school group felt that they could achieve whatever they set their mind to (question 3) compared to 15 per cent of the INSET group, which indicates an internal locus of control. It has been found that people who identify their locus of control as within themselves experience less stress. The school sample tended to respond in a far more empowered way with an internal locus of control, and not as victims of chance. A total of 75 per cent of the INSET group relied more on chance.

Three 'yes/no' questions were asked concerning role factors: whether the teachers thought they could influence decisions which directly affected them; whether they were asked to undertake tasks that conflict; and whether they had enough time to undertake those tasks they considered they should do? One curious finding is that 82 per cent of the INSET group said that they could influence decisions compared to 69 per cent of the school group. This is inconsistent with the findings in the locus of control section. This is even more interesting when considering the number who experienced role conflict (48 per cent of the INSET group and 28 per cent of the school group). It is possible that they have to argue the case in order to avoid conflicting demands and are thus more fully involved in the decision-making process. The school group also expressed confidence in their colleagues' competence (question 2), which was not shared by the INSET group. This gives an impression of the school as an arena in which the teacher moves confidently with an assurance of professionalism. In contrast, the INSET group were not confident within their settings, expressing a lack of confidence in their colleagues' competence, and the organization and management of the schools. They also give the impression of lacking self-confidence, of a confused role with colleagues in whom they lack confidence, and a lack of communication and cooperation (question 4), although they claim empowerment in decision making.

Within the school, the teachers are clearly challenged by the special needs pupils, and lack confidence in their teaching approach. An indirect expression of this challenge is in the lack of satisfaction in resources available. Although the INSET group were especially dissatisfied, this may be explained by their knowledge of a multiplicity of resources developed during their courses, and the realization that their special needs pupils were being sold short. More books and resources were ranked third by the school group and fifth by the INSET group in the factors to relieve pressure, and the teachers in the school felt a lack of suitable teaching materials for the special needs pupils. A reduction in class size and an increase in staff were both considered to be important in reducing pressure, and would perhaps have an implied effect on enabling teachers to spend more time with children with learning difficulties. The INSET group does not appear to be as challenged by the pupils themselves, but rather by the challenge of the schools which their courses have led them to be more critical of, through an awareness of new idealism.

The major differences between the two groups is in the social settings of their work. While both groups wanted smaller classes and more resources, including staff, the INSET group were looking for structural alterations within the school organization and were less concerned with improving discipline, or more time. Some of these differences can perhaps be explained in the current rhetoric of special educational needs and the development of whole-school approaches, with the special needs teacher as a co-ordinator of support rather than a remedial teacher. The school sample were more concerned with survival and being able to do a good job by having more time.

The teachers were asked to list their concerns in priority. The school sample showed different priorities from the INSET group, in that the teachers in the school were reality orientated, and they showed concern for their pupils above all, for their professional tasks in terms of doing a good job within the organization of the school and for the time available. The INSET group, on the other hand, were not classroom orientated, but again were concerned above all with the organization of the school and their own roles within it, with pupils coming third in their ranking. Both groups were very concerned about the adequacy of the school(s) in relation to pupils with special needs, and the social effects on the pupils.

An important buffer to stress is social support. One of the most important ways to facilitate coping and reduce stress is to provide an appropriate caring management structure which enables support systems to operate, by providing time for staff to support each other. The school group appeared quite satisfied with the management of their school, but the INSET group were not. However, the INSET group reported more social support, in spite of the potential stress arising from incompetent colleagues.

The school group of teachers appear to feel more autonomy. For example, 60 per cent were satisfied with their curriculum compared to only 19 per cent of the INSET group. Additionally, the teachers in the school felt self-empowered and identified themselves as having an internal locus of control, whereas the INSET group felt themselves to be more like victims of external loci of control. This is contradicted by their involvement in decision-making which directly affects them (82 per cent indicated that they were involved compared to 69 per cent of the teachers in the school group). However, the INSET group also experienced more conflicting demands (48 per cent compared to 28 per cent of the school sample).

Summary and conclusions

In this paper, I have discussed the development of idealism in initial teacher education as the socialization into a profession with shared meanings and assumptions about good teachers. These aspects also appear to be characteristic of full-time INSET courses, with strong rhetorical consequences. A model of teacher stress is briefly described which seeks to offer one explanation for the way that teachers appraise themselves as stressed within the social context of the school. This model uses the two levels of coping and the threshold between them to illuminate the variability in coping which individuals experience. Three aspects of teaching were put forward as factors which had been found to influence strongly the appraisal process – autonomy, competence and satisfaction. The findings of a small study were presented to illustrate the contentions made, and the way that the full-time INSET courses change teachers' perceptions of themselves.

Teachers are challenged by pupils with special educational needs in the school, even if they have confidence in the management of the school and their colleagues. They feel their competence challenged, and they feel a need for additional support. They also expressed concerns about the overall adequacy of the schooling received by those children they defined as having special needs. This is an important finding in a study which found that on the whole teachers are satisfied with their own performance as teachers. Even those teachers thought of by their colleagues as the experts (the INSET group), expressed doubts about their own ability to teach the children with special needs, given the inadequacy of the schools.

The question to ask is who are going to be more stressed – the teachers who are reality based, acknowledge inefficiency but feel professionally supported, or those who are idealistic in their outlook, are concerned about the management of their schools and consider their colleagues to be incompetent? This can be considered within the model presented earlier. The teachers in the school are able to concentrate on their teaching because they are professionally supported, and this will enable coping to be on the whole at the EMPLOYEE level, with a threshold between BOSS and EMPLOYEE which is relatively high. Those who are idealistic will experience conflicting demands and inappropriate demands being made on them, which do not fit into their legitimated tasks or are thrust upon them through the incompetence of colleagues. These teachers perceive schools as essentially hostile places for the children they wish to protect, within a society which is also uncaring. All of these aspects of work will influence the appraisal process and affect their experience of work as stressful, including the level of their thresholds between the BOSS and EMPLOYEE levels of coping. The fundamental aspect is that if coping is at BOSS level, the person is conscious of stress and not coping, in addition to BOSS having a limited capacity. This limited capacity can lead to additional problems in occupations such as teaching, which rely on 'thinking on your feet'.

The implications for INSET providers are many, but perhaps the most important is that although resocialization may be inevitable, the link between rhetoric and reality must be made, otherwise teachers from full-time INSET courses are likely to return to school and experience increased amounts of stress. For teachers who are already challenged by children with special educational needs, the additional problem of developing idealism which may lead to assumptions about new rituals to magic problems away, may increase the experience of stress to an intolerable level. Another problem for teachers returning to their school from a full-time course is that the social support systems previously experienced may no longer exist, the social climate of the school may have changed, the cook book of solutions may include new recipes, and different power groups may exist. Teachers often find positive resistance to their idealism, with their colleagues expecting jargonized talk and new simplistic rituals to cure all ills. The teacher returning from a full-time course has also developed different shared meanings within the student group and tutors.

The current move towards courses which are more school-focused, or where practical work in schools alongside the theoretical and practical aspects of the work in the institution is required, would appear to offer opportunities for teachers to develop a critical analysis without taking them totally outside the classroom.

References

Apple, M. (1979). *Ideology and Curriculum.* Routledge and Kegan Paul: London.

Caplan, G. and Killelea, M. (eds) (1976). *Support Systems and Mutual Help: Multidisciplinary Explorations.* Grune and Stratton: London.

Cruichshank, D., Kennedy, J. and Myers, B. (1974). Perceived problems of secondary school teachers. *Journal of Educational Research* **68**, 154–9.

Dodgson, H. (1987). Ritual in a reception class – an ethnographic study. Unpublished M.Ed. dissertation, University of Liverpool, Liverpool.

Dunham, J. (1984). *Stress in Teaching.* Croom Helm: London.

Edelman, M. (1977). *Political Language: Words that Succeed and Policies that Fail.* Academic Press: London and San Diego.

Fletcher, B. and Payne, R. (1982). Levels of reported stressors and strains amongst school teachers: some UK data. *Educational Review* **34**(3), 267–78.

Freeman, A. (1986). Coping in schools: A case study of teacher stress and coping in a secondary school. Unpublished Ph.D. thesis, University of Sheffield, Sheffield.

Freeman, A. (1987). The coping teacher. *Research in Education* **38**, 1–16.

Freeman, A. (1988). Parents: Dilemmas for professionals. *Disability Handicap and Society* **3**(1), 79–85.

Freeman, A. (in press). Stress and coping: The idea of threshold. *Child and Educational Psychology.*

Haan, N. (1977). *Coping and Defending: Processes of Self-environmental Organisation.* Academic Press: London and San Diego.

Harris, K. (1982). *Teachers and Classes: A Marxist Analysis*. Routledge and Kegan Paul: London.

Kyriacou, C. and Sutcliffe, J. (1979). A note on teacher stress and locus of control. *Journal of Occupational Psychology* **52**, 227–8.

Lortie, D. C. (1975). *School Teacher*. University of Chicago Press: Chicago.

Morris, P. (1981). The cognitive psychology of self reports. In Antaki, C. (ed.), *The Psychology of Ordinary Explanations of Social Behaviour*. Academic Press: London and San Diego.

Payne, R. (1974). *Social Priority, Vol. 2: E.P.A. Surveys and Statistics*. HMSO: London.

Pettegrew, L. and Wolf, G. (1982). Validating measures of teacher stress. *American Educational Research Journal* **19**(3), 373–96 (Autumn).

Pollard, A. (1980). Teacher interests and changing situations of survival threat in primary school classrooms. In Woods, P. (ed.), *Teacher Strategies*. Croom Helm: London.

Simpson, P. (1972). Special teaching – special training. *Forward Trends* (July), 58–61.

Stensrud, R. and Stensrud, K. (1983). Coping skills training: A systematic approach to stress management counselling. *The Personnel and Guidance Journal* **62D**, 214–18.

Woods, P. (1979). *The Divided School*. Routledge and Kegan Paul: London.

MENTAL HEALTH AMONG SCHOOL TEACHERS

Binoy Chakravorty

Introduction

Deterioration of mental health in the general population is a growing problem. A total of 5 million people in England alone (10.9 per cent of the population) consult their general practitioners each year about mental health problems! Of these, 600 000 (1.3 per cent) utilize specialist psychiatric services, and 110 000 hospital beds are in use for psychiatric treatment. A national survey estimates that on average in industry 40 million working days per year are lost through symptoms related to mental ill health – four times the amount lost through industrial action. The problem is also becoming equally serious among teachers. On the basis of research from all over Europe and the United States a recent ILO report recognizes stress as an 'occupational disease' among teachers.

While analysing the causes of prolonged sickness absences among the school teachers of an education authority it became evident that prolonged sickness absence, though not common among school teachers, was, when it did occur, most commonly caused by psychiatric illness. This roused my attention and interest and the purpose of this paper is to analyse the problem, and see how much of this can be remedied by timely intervention. In such instances, the absences usually continued for 2–4 years, and even with medical care the majority of cases resulted in resignation or early retirement. In general, the effect is a temporary or permanent loss of expensively-trained professional staff leading to the disruption of teaching in schools. A new teacher cannot be appointed until a final decision is made, which may take a few years. In the meantime, the gap is filled by the teacher's colleagues, or on rare occasions with a supply teacher if the school is fortunate enough to get one. Above all there is a substantial wastage of human and national resources.

In most cases of long sickness absence the cause is some form of mental illness; this may range from anxiety, irritability, nervous debility, depression, or a combination of obsession, mania, and panicky reactions. Drinking problems have been noted in a small minority of absentees. Psychiatric consultant care was needed in each case and the outcome, judging from the ability to return to normal teaching duties, was very poor. In a small number there were associated physical illnesses or personal and family problems, which possibly added to, or precipitated, the inability to cope, which later led to overt psychiatric illness.

Teachers are considered an important professional group in the community, and the aim of this study is to attempt to understand why mental illness is the most common cause of early invalidity in teachers, and to examine suggestions which may help to prevent this happening.

Subjects and methods

The present study was based on the observation of prolonged sickness absence in a total of 1552 teachers. There were 43 cases of prolonged sickness absence ranging from 2 to 4 years during 1974–83, and psychiatric disorders were responsible for 33 (77 per cent) of them.

The types of disorders identified included nervous breakdown resulting from depression with or without anxiety and obsession, behavioural problems, and alcoholism. Stress was found to play a significant part in contributing to the mental problems in most cases (being associated with difficulties and dissatisfaction at work, involving relationships with both colleagues and pupils, with family problems, and with the presence of organic disease). Of those suffering from mental ill health, 21 (64 per cent) had to retire or resign early and discontinue teaching.

Since the 1974 reorganization of the Health Service, district local authority medical matters have come under the domain of district health authorities. This arrangement, in fact, was of great help to this study, because case histories and files were available from the records section of the Community Services. Extensive cooperation was obtained from the personnel section of the education authority for the past histories, and subsequent follow-up study of the effect of diseases on job performance, and any further recurrence of the illnesses. Hospital consultants' opinions were obtained in all cases from the correspondence contained in the files between the community medical officer and various general practitioners and consultants under whose care the absentee teachers were. The records were very informative, which is possibly due to the existing education authority regulations that any teachers absenting themselves for more than 3 months on the grounds of mental illness are suspended from duty, and a psychiatric opinion is usually necessary when returning to work certifying fitness to teach children. In 33 of these prolonged absences the responsible cause was a psychiatric illness, while in 10 cases ailments were varied.

The category of schools and the socio-economic backgrounds of the pupils of those schools concerned were examined to see if they were associated with the teachers' mental states. Consideration was also given to the teaching of adolescent remedial, or educationally subnormal, children in order to examine whether such teachers were more likely than other teachers to suffer from mental ill health.

A detailed history of each teacher's case was examined to find any contributory or associated cause (e.g. physical illness, domestic or work problems), stressful life events (e.g. the death of a near or dear one, marriage, the birth of a child), enforced changes in working conditions, etc., which were recorded with dates, especially those taking place within the past 1–2 years.

Age, sex, and their relation with mental well-being were considered. Factors specific to women were also noted, e.g. association of menopause, and role-strain, if any, due to sex-role stereotyping. Family histories were examined for any associated hereditary influences. Problems arising within the work area were critically examined from all aspects, e.g. physical, administrative or those involving relationships with pupils or colleagues.

In addition to reports from general practitioners and hospital consultants, every absentee teacher had a medical examination by one of the community medical officers following the routine local authority request and, in addition, they had to fill in one 'General Health Questionnaire' form after the final decision was made. A follow-up examination was also made to assess the teacher's ability to return to his or her own job. Details of medicines, shock treatment, laboratory investigations, etc., were excluded from this study. A summary of the findings for each absentee teacher was recorded on individual index cards to facilitate the study.

To find out whether the teachers of schools containing more pupils from lower socio-economic groups were more vulnerable to mental illness, a study was made of the demand for 'free' school meals in different schools, but there was no definite relation, i.e. the incidence of mental illness among teachers was independent of this measure of the socio-economic class of the pupils.

A control group of teachers who are at present 'in employment' was identified, keeping their age, sex, marital status, and type of school in common with the 'cases', i.e. the teachers who have already retired on grounds of mental ill health. The same questionnaire with a little modification was sent to them for a 'case control' study.

Results

In a total of 1552 teachers studied, there were 43 cases of prolonged sickness absence ranging from 2 to 4 years during 1974–83. In 10 of these 43 cases, ailments were varied, but in the remaining 33 cases, the cause was due to psychiatric disorders. The types of disorders identified included nervous breakdown, resulting from depression with or without anxiety and obsession, behavioural problems and alcoholism (Table 3.3).

Although the size and means of recruiting the sample of 33 teachers make it impossible to generalize with certainty, there is a suggestion that both the type of school and the teacher's age may be related to the

Table 3.3 Mental health among school teachers.

	No. of teachers	
Illness	Male	Female
Depression with nervous breakdown	2	15
Depression with anxiety states	3	2 (1 with agitation)
Depression with anxiety states and obsession	2	—
Depression with maniacal reaction	3	1
Behavioural problems	2 (1 with violence to children; 1 with lapse of memory)	1
Alcoholism	1	1 (with agitation)
Total	13	20

incidence of psychiatric disorder. Overall, gender did not, however, appear to be significant. With regard to the type of school, it appeared that teachers in special schools and remedial classes may be particularly prone to stress-related illnesses, whereas sixth-form teachers seemed to be less susceptible. As far as age was concerned, there seemed to be a tendency for women in their 40s, and men in their 20s and 40s, to be more susceptible.

For each of the teachers with a psychiatric illness, treatment by a hospital consultant was necessary, though the ultimate results were far from satisfactory. Of the 33 teachers in question, 21 had to leave the teaching profession – 13 retired on the grounds of ill health and 8 resigned – but 10 have since returned to work and still continue to teach, 4 in a different situation, occupying positions with less responsibility. In the remaining case no decision has yet been reached – it is the third year of her absence.

One woman teacher who was teaching in a special school had been suffering from ulcerative colitis for several years. At 46 she started showing behaviour and personality disorders and came under psychiatric care. After 3 years of treatment there was no improvement and she became severely depressed. A colectomy was decided on by surgical colleagues to improve her condition, but unfortunately she did not live long after the operation.

For some of these teachers I could find background causes which possibly played a major contributory role. It is probable that there were similar cases, but a thorough case history was not always available – more so when there were difficulties with colleagues or superiors. However, some underlying factors were identified in about 85 per cent (28 of 33) of the absent teachers (see Fig. 3.3).

Two teachers (one male, one female) reported drink problems, though there is doubt whether their alcoholism was a cause or effect of a depressive illness. Five (one male, four female) had physical illnesses (ulcerative colitis, angina, deafness, prostatic hypertrophy). In seven cases (one male, six female), there were domestic problems, including marital discord, long illness of the husband, long illness of the mother, problems with the son, death of the mother abroad. School problems appeared to be crucial in 18 cases (nine male, nine female), which included difficulties with senior colleagues, loss of confidence, disruptive pupils, effects of resource cuts, low pay, and anxieties caused by promotion, redeployment, job loss and new challenges.

In this analysis of contributory factors some examples of case histories will be used within the limits of confidentiality.

Most of the 33 teachers were married, and had a family; only 4 of the male and 4 of the female teachers remained single. Whereas a happily married family is a supportive agent in mitigating the effects of stress,

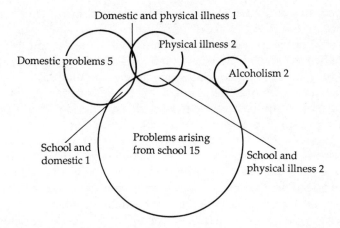

Fig. 3.3 Analysis of contributory factors.

unhappiness in the family, arising from the husband–wife relationship, or from children, is detrimental. In our study, three women teachers had marital difficulties, their marriages ending in divorce. In one of them there was an additional problem with a grown-up son who was involved with the police. In another two, there were histories of long-term strain where the husbands suffered from prolonged illness before they were widowed.

Stress in a family may originate not only from marriage and children but also from other sources. One of the teachers lives with his mother and has been looking after her for years; she is incontinent with senile dementia. The teacher is unmarried and looks after his mother without the support of anyone else. Another woman teacher lived with her mother who went on a holiday abroad where she died. The teacher felt helpless, and it became too much trouble to arrange for the preparation needed for her mother's burial. She was still coping, until she was involved in a car accident in which several people were hurt. The combined effect of all these 'events' was too much for her and shortly afterwards she went into agitated depression.

One of the single women teachers, aged 48, developed depression with behavioural disorders, and an examination later revealed that she had total sensory deafness in one ear and partial deafness in the other. She had been hiding her disability for many years and now felt insecure and started worrying about her dependency, which resulted in behavioural problems.

It is not yet certain whether psychiatric illnesses have any genetic influence, but the personality and behaviour patterns of parents may influence their children. In one teacher there was a history of mental illness in his father, mother and one cousin. He is a 30-year-old bachelor, and since his father died 2 years ago he has been living with his mother and grandmother. After 3 years of illness he has now returned to work.

Physical illnesses, especially chronic ones, have definite bearings on mental health. Two of the women teachers had suffered from ulcerative colitis, one of whom died following surgery. In another, complaints of angina started before the mental symptoms appeared. One of the male teachers suffered from chronic urinary retention due to prostatic hypertrophy and later went into manic depression.

Situations arising from school were varied, either arising from teaching children, or from administration. It is known that the teaching of sub-normal and maladjusted children, and occasionally adolescents, may be stressful, but in this study only one single male teacher of 29 had complained of stress with adolescent teaching. Another high school teacher of 31 lost his confidence in teaching, and started blaming himself because he had chosen the wrong profession. In two other male teachers, aged 25 and 41, the consultant's report stated that they were lacking in their ability to match up to the normal stress and strain of teaching. The younger one resigned, and the other opted for retirement. Two of the married high school women teachers (aged 41 and 45) after several years of experience expressed a loss of confidence in teaching.

Problems with the headteacher, or deputy head, figured prominently as one of the underlying stressful factors. Four male and four female teachers complained of their deteriorating relationships with them. They were thought to be over-critical, less understanding, and too distant from their colleagues.

During this study it was noted that the peak incidence of mental illness among teachers occurred in 1979. There was also an increase in 1982–3 over 1980–81 (see Fig. 3.4). These two periods coincided with two administrative reorganizations. In September 1979 the grammar and secondary schools were reorganized into high schools and sixth form colleges, and in September 1983 there was an amalgamation of schools – in the district studied, four high schools combined to form two, and two primary schools merged into one.

During and preceding these reorganizations the teachers underwent a lot of stress. In the first reorganization many teachers had to reapply for their jobs; for many, the subjects they had been teaching changed, and they felt that their promotion had been bypassed. In both of these reorganizations, probably no teacher lost his or her job, but some had to move to schools in different areas and, therefore, move home as well. Some had to rearrange their children's schools, wife's job, etc. Many nearing the age of retirement reluctantly chose to retire, and some resigned.

On the whole, most of them passed through prolonged stages of uncertainty, tension and apprehension, which in some resulted in

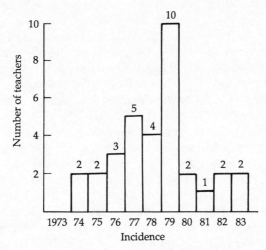

Fig. 3.4 Incidence of mental illness among school teachers.

anxiety states leading to depression. Such a history was obtained in four of our male and five of our female teachers.

Such anxieties sometimes added to the existing stress leading to breakdown. One of the women teachers on an outing to a National Park temporarily lost contact with the children and panicked, and the media got hold of the news before she was reunited with the children. She was very upset at this coverage but took it calmly. Shortly after came the 1979 reorganization. She was required to teach a subject that was not her speciality, and her promotion, she felt, was bypassed. Within a few weeks, this resulted in a state of anxiety and depression, but following treatment for 3 years, she is now back at work and has been redeployed to another school.

Discussion

Like any other problem, if the source can be identified, the answer to the problem becomes easier. In this case it is very difficult to find the source when there are so many abstract factors influencing the situation. In one word, the source of the problem is 'stress'. Human psyche is an undefinable and unestimable factor which is inherent to the individual. On this depends one's behaviour pattern, social relations, reaction to the environment and, most important, one's capacity to cope with stress. Individual differences in style may explain why some people appear to cope better with stress than others. Occupational differences also affect individual coping reactions.

It was noted that there was a preponderance of female teachers in the 40–50 age group. The Oxford investigation (Bungay *et al.*, 1980) has shown that irritability, difficulty in making decisions, and loss of confidence are more common in this age group. In men, irritability usually appears in the 35–40 and 55–60 age groups. The other two symptoms, i.e. difficulty in making decisions and loss of confidence, usually make their appearance after age 50. It can be assumed, as a rule, that middle life is a vulnerable time for all of us.

In men, and occasionally in careerist women, this may be a time for a sort of 'stock taking', i.e. self-appraisal and reflection about one's own achievements and failures. Although mortgages might have been paid up, children have grown up, and financial situations have improved, this self-evaluation 'balance sheet' may show that only certain ambitions have been achieved and a sense of disappointment or failure may supervene. Marital stress is also not uncommon at this age, with a feeling of neglect by one's partner or union with a partner of a much lower age. Children usually leave home at this time: the additive effect of these factors may precipitate depression in certain individuals.

Younger teachers, i.e. between 20 and 29 years of age, show signs of stress when they develop a feeling of inadequacy, and start thinking that teaching is probably not the right profession for them. Difficulties arising from romantic involvements, marriage, new parenthood, house mortgages, insufficient earnings, etc., either singly or in combination add to the stress situation in young teachers.

Simpson (1976) undertook a similar study of sickness absence among teachers and, in his opinion, much of their illnesses were directly related to stress. He was able to show an increased incidence of sickness absence, in men in age groups 20–34 and 55–64, whereas in women it was in the 40–54 age group. The present study presents a similar picture.

At the end of a long period of absence the male teachers tended to resign more often than their female colleagues, who preferred retirement on medical grounds. This may be that men are able to find more suitable jobs, whereas women prefer to settle down with their pension.

Adaptation to stress varies. Some people are able to withstand a far greater degree of stress than others, depending upon their attitude, personality and past experience. Brown and Harris (1978), Holmes and Rahe (1967) and many other workers observed a strong association between 'life events', physical disease and psychological illness; they postulated that significant life events could precipitate disease. Every event can be given a 'score' and when added together can give a cumulative effect. These events may not always be unpleasant, e.g. events like marriage, the birth of a child, or acceptance of a new job, may all be the starting point for psychological stress. Eastwood and Trevelyan

(1972) believed stressful conditions could originate illness by first producing a psychological disease. In 12 of the teachers observed, we were able to associate physical illness with domestic frustration. Aetiological factors such as ulcerative colitis and ischaemic heart disease have long been linked with stress (see Lidermann, 1950; Osler, 1974).

When multiple events take place within a short time interval, or there is an associated physical illness or domestic problem, coping becomes difficult and often results in nervous breakdown. Retrospective studies of psychiatric patients have shown that they had a greater experience of stressful life events compared to the general population (see, e.g. Murphy and Brown, 1980). In three of the teachers bereavement in the family acted as a stressful event and probably precipitated nervous breakdown. The recent death of near and dear ones has been described by Parkes (1964) and Birtchnell (1970) as precipitating mental ill health. Bereavement in the family may result in mental illness, especially when combined with other stressful events. However, in one of the two teachers who had suffered from depressive illness following the chronic suffering of their husbands, death of the husband brought relief; she improved, returned to her job, and is now remarried and settled. The death of a near one may sometimes serve to resolve a chronic stress situation.

Influence of behavioural patterns

Lader's (1971) elaborate research on mental illness and psychosomatic disease has greatly increased our appreciation of 'anxiety states'. He felt that there was a reciprocal correlation between 'habituation' and anxiety. Poor habituation, which is usual with 'introverts', leads to anxiety. On the other hand, 'extroverts', who focus their attention more on the outside world and less on their subjective feelings, habituate more readily, and are less likely to go into an anxiety state.

Friedman and Rosenman (1974) described the influence of behaviour patterns in precipitating coronary heart disease; they inferred that persons showing intense ambition, competitive drive, constant preoccupation, and always with a sense of urgency (identified as type 'A', and those not having such behaviour as type 'B') were more prone to coronary diseases. This observation has been supported by subsequent workers (Heller, 1978; Quinn and Bloom, 1978), but none has yet drawn any association of mental illness with such behaviour patterns.

In this study I have observed that even with medical care, two-thirds of the teachers suffering from mental illness dropped out after a long-term sickness absence which resulted in nervous breakdown. Kyriacou and Pratt (1985), in a study of 127 school teachers, observed an association between teacher stress and psychosomatic symptoms which appeared to be greatest in the areas of anxiety, somatic and depressive symptoms.

Approaches to reducing stress

There appear to be two main approaches towards solving this problem – to prevent it happening, and to treat the person when it has happened. Prevention should be aimed, first, at removing, alleviating or modifying the factors causing stress and, secondly, at preparing the individual for coping with it.

However, one question still remains unanswered – why does it happen to some but not to others undergoing similar 'stress' situations? In our 'case control' study, we identified some 'control' teachers who had undergone similar job stresses, including the uncertainties of reorganization and similar difficult 'life events' to the 'cases', but they coped very well and continue as teachers. This brings us to the question of 'man–job fitness', i.e. identifying a person as suitable for the job. Cox (1978) refers to two kinds of fitness; the first is to see how much the person's abilities and skills match the demands and requirements of the job and its environment, and the second is to note how far his or her internal needs, values and desires are being satisfied. Whenever there is a 'poor fit' of either kind there is low job satisfaction and difficulties will arise. Gradually, it may lead to anxiety, depression or mental illness.

Psychologists maintain that they can identify 'at risk' persons by appropriate psychometric testing and subjective assessments. The 'poor risk' person may not be selected for the job, but borderline people can be suitably trained either before they start, or by in-service training. Inadequately trained workers show more stress in work situations.

Psychometric testing before entering teacher training, if used alone, or if its results are subject to interpretation by untrained persons, will probably not be suitable as an instrument for the selection and assessment of teachers. On the other hand, a pre-employment interview by a psychologist may be of great help in the assessment, in addition to a physical examination. At interview the psychologist can analyse the prospective teacher's past and immediate past life events, and count the total scores to judge his or her adaptability to stress, and ability to cope. In other words, the psychologist's skills in clinical judgement will add considerably to the 'test-specific' data which are obtained by standardized psychometric testing. The predictive validity of personality questionnaires (and other psychometric assessment instruments) is recognized as less than perfect; a skilled interviewer, however, can assess an individual's abilities to cope with major life events, with real or hypothetical stressors, and will make judgements and inferences about the person's future performance by reference to his present and past experience, rather than by comparing the individual with a 'normative' sample.

If psychological assessment is carried out before entry into teacher training, and the results show that the degree of incompatibility may not be improved with training, the person should be advised to opt for a different career. It is always wise to undertake a different occupation at the start, rather than waiting to find out that one is not suited to one's chosen profession.

Once trained, teachers would be less likely to experience stress if there were better communications and cohesion between colleagues at all levels. When there are possibilities of a reorganization or amalgamation which may result in job losses or transfers, or changes in teachers' status or promotion prospects, teachers are much better able to cope with the situation if they know what to expect: they then have time to mobilize their physical, psychological and material resources to cope with the eventualities. Seligman (1975) has pointed out that when events are seen by individuals to be unpredictable, they perceive a sense of anxiety, and when they consider them as uncontrollable, a feeling of helplessness akin to depression sets in. Individuals experience breakdown when something happens for which they are not at all prepared. Egbert et al. (1964) showed that among patients waiting for abdominal surgery, those who had been informed how they would feel after the operation, where they would feel pain, how long it would last, and how severe it would be, experienced much less anxiety, were more comfortable and required fewer narcotics compared to others who had no such preoperative discussion. Egbert et al. felt this was the effect of good doctor–patient communication.

At school there should be an active endeavour to break down the communication barrier. Talking over problems with colleagues is a big step towards a reduction of work stress, and the mutual sharing of experience, even of apprehension, boosts one's morale and gives a feeling of 'I am not alone'. Support is an essential item in stress reduction; problems should be discussed not only with colleagues and friends but also with one's spouse and friendly family members. There is a good deal of truth in the aphorism 'a problem shared is a problem halved'.

According to Groen (1971), stress is more common in an unhealthy organization which 'consists of people who instead of giving each other unconditional mutual support become rivals and have to work and communicate with each other in situations of ambivalence, distrust and conflict'. He also adds that interpersonal conflicts about authority relationships at work are related to the development of coronary diseases.

Promotion prospects also cause stress among teachers; it might be useful to have definite criteria for promotion, and these may be tactfully discussed to dispense with any feeling of nepotism or injustice. The 'whys' in promotion should be explained beforehand so that one can estimate one's own prospects to some extent.

Other chapters in this volume describe some of the strategies individuals can adopt to cope with stress. It is doubtful, however, whether anyone develops immunity to stress: coping successfully with a series of smaller stressful events in life does not necessarily help when a major crisis occurs. On the contrary, a cumulative process seems to occur with aggregated stress, possibly resulting in nervous breakdown.

Intervention is necessary when signs of stress begin to show as anxiety, tiredness, sleeplessness, irritability, hesitancy to take decisions, repeated sickness absences, etc. Here one's spouse, colleagues and friends are of immense importance. They may sense something is wrong and advise the teacher to seek help. Help, as has already been seen, may not always be medical – it may be social, domestic or administrative, varying according to the source of stress. Supporting advice and good counselling may be all that is required initially, and a doctor may be more important as a source of this support than as a supplier of tablets. However, doctors may sometimes issue short-term sick notes to help teachers under great stress to withdraw temporarily, and to give them the opportunity to regain the capacity to withstand such stress; it acts as a small premium against a future prolonged absence or withdrawal from the profession.

Conclusion

Occupational stress has come to be recognized as a major economic cost. Even during the industrial strife of 1974 the *Financial Times* argued that 'stress costs more than strikes'.

In the present day, teaching is undoubtedly a stressful occupation, and it will never be possible to get rid of stress from work completely. So the aim should be to attempt to reduce it, and prepare people at the receiving end to cope with it more successfully. Proper selection and training procedures for teachers according to 'school fitness', early recognition of stress symptoms, and a timely intervention may save a substantial drain on human and national resources. In cases where a return to teaching is impossible, and termination on medical grounds becomes imperative, sympathetic consideration should be given to compensation and benefits.

According to the definition of the World Health Organization (1950):

Occupational Health should aim at the promotion and maintenance of the highest degree of physical, mental and social well-being of workers in all occupations; . . . the protection of workers in their

employment from risks adverse to health; the placing and maintenance in an occupational environment adapted to his physiological
and psychological equipment; and to summarise the adaptation of
work to man and of each man to his job.

We have still a long way to go but, nevertheless, we must strive for these
goals.

References

Birtchnell, J. (1970). Recent parent death and mental illness. *British Journal of Psychiatry* **116**, 282–97.

Brown, G. W. and Harris, T. (1978). *Social Origin of Depression*. Tavistock: London.

Bungay, G. T., Vessey, M. P. and McPherson, C. K. (1980). Study of symptoms in middle life with special reference to the menopause. *British Medical Journal* **I**, 181–3.

Cox, T. (1978). *Stress*, pp. 168–73. Macmillan: London.

Eastwood, M. R. and Trevelyan, H. (1972). The relationship between physical and psychiatric disorder. *Psychosomatic Medicine* **34**, 363–72.

Egbert, L., Battit, G., Welch, C. and Bartlett, M. (1964). Reduction of postoperative pain by encouragement and instruction of patients. *New England Journal of Medicine* **270**, 825–7.

Financial Times (1974) 28 April.

Friedman, M. and Rosenman, R. H. (1959). Association of overt behaviour pattern with blood and cardiovascular findings – blood cholesterol level, blood clotting time, incidence of arcus senilis, and clinical coronary artery disease. *Journal of the American Medical Association* **169**(12), 1286–96.

Friedman, M. and Rosenman, R. H. (1974). *Type A Behaviour and Your Heart*. Knopf: New York.

Groen, J. J. (1971). Social change and psychosomatic disease. In Levi, L. (ed.), *Society, Stress and Disease*. Oxford University Press: Oxford.

Heller, R. F. (1978). Type A behaviour and coronary heart disease. *British Medical Journal* **2**, 368.

Holmes, T. H. and Rahe, R. H. (1967). The social readjustment rating scale. *Journal of Psychosomatic Research* **11**, 213–18.

Kyriacou, C. and Pratt, J. (1985). Teacher stress and psychoneurotic symptoms. *British Journal of Educational Psychology* **55**, 61–4.

Lader, M. H. (1971). The responses of normal subjects and psychiatric patients to repetitive stimulation. In Levi, L. (ed.), *Society, Stress and Disease*. Oxford University Press: Oxford.

Lidermann, E. (1950). Modifications in the course of ulcerative colitis in relation to change in life situations and reaction patterns. *American Review of Neurological and Mental Disease Proceedings* **29**, 706–23.

Murphy, E. and Brown, J. H. (1980). Life events, psychiatric disturbance and physical illness. *British Journal of Psychiatry* **136**, 326–38.

Osler, W. (1974). The effect of exposure to culture change, social change, and change in interpersonal relationship on health (quoted by Hinkle, L. E., Jr). In Dohrenwend, R. S. and Dohrenwend, B. P. (eds), *Stressful Life Events: Their Nature and Effects*. Wiley: New York.

Parkes, C. M. (1964). Recent bereavement as a cause of mental illness. *British Journal of Psychiatry* **110**, 198.

Quinn, R. M. and Bloom L. J. (1978). Anxiety management training for pattern A behaviour. *Journal of Behavioural Medicine* **I**, 25–36.

Seligman, M. E. P. (1975). *Depression, Development and Death*. W. H. Freeman: San Francisco.

Simpson, J. (1976). Stress, sickness absence and teachers. In NASUWT (ed.), *Stress in Schools*, pp. 11–17. National Association of Schoolmasters and Union of Women Teachers: Hemel Hempstead.

World Health Organization (1950). *Bulletin on Occupational Health*. WHO: Geneva.

4 STRESS AND THE SOCIAL CONTEXT

Comment: You don't have to be mad to be a teacher, but it certainly helps.

There are times when teachers seem to be a bit crazy – not in the eyes of their pupils or of parents, but to each other. There can be very few of them who cannot recall having seen or shared in those unrehearsed and startling occasions in the staffroom in which normally serious and sensitive people get swept up into routines of high farce, manic satire or genuine horseplay – mocking school rituals, ridiculing the formal or elaborating the in-joke. In a discussion of humour in school published elsewhere, Peter Woods, the author of the following chapter, has pointed to the significance of this superficially trivial behaviour. 'Laughter,' he suggests, 'is the coping mechanism par excellence. Lack of it might suggest non-survival. Its presence is a sure indication of managing.'

This chapter by Woods is not about laughter. But to note its significance serves to point to an important element in our consideration of teaching and stress. If laughter, serving as a kind of release or reaction to tension, is a routine feature of teachers' lives in school, so are the pressures which generate it. In short, stress is an endemic feature of teaching. In the discussion which follows, Woods identifies some of the basic characteristics of how teaching and the role of the teacher are defined in ways which are inherently stressful. This is important. First, because it forces us to look again at how different individuals respond to cultural expectations about the role of the teacher, in ways which either magnify or contain inherently stressful features of the work. Secondly, because it allows us to consider how changes in definitions of the teacher's role – especially those emanating from outside of teaching or the culture of teachers – are also likely to change both the degree of stress endemic to teaching and the mechanisms available for teachers to cope with this aspect of their work.

STRESS AND THE TEACHER ROLE

Peter Woods

A high risk of stress appears to be an inherent feature of the teacher's job. It is hardly surprising, given its nature. Waller (1932) has described teaching as being basically conflictual, Berlack and Berlack (1981) as dilemma-ridden, and Hargreaves (1988) as constrained by factors beyond an individual teacher's control. There are also tortuous problems connected with the teacher role, i.e. the position a teacher occupies in a school and the expectations that people (including the teacher) have of what should or should not be done in it. There was at one time quite a trend in studies of teachers and role conflict (e.g. Grace, 1972). It might be fruitful to reconsider this in the light of the prevailing interest in teacher stress, and of recent and current developments in education. 'Stress', of course, is a psychological state; but it is precipitated largely, I would argue, by social factors.

A model of stress

Kyriacou (1987, p. 146; Chapter 2, this volume) has suggested that 'stress' is 'the experience by a teacher of unpleasant emotions, such as tension, frustration, anxiety, anger and depression, resulting from aspects of work as a teacher'. There are times, however, when tension, anxiety, even anger can be quite productive, and frustration is part of the cost of living in society. At the very least, we must say that these are no ordinary tensions and anxieties such as would go with our own perceptions of the role. Teachers experiencing stress are ones driven to the limits of their personal resources, where they hover on the brink of breakdown.

If this is the psychological product, the immediate cause in many cases, as I see it, is a disjuncture or maladjustment of two or more factors that normally might be expected to work in harmony. It is not just pressures, therefore, which some may need in order to function; nor problems, which are a necessary part of a professional's job. An alternative view is of the 'ordinary' course of events, as one exhibiting a dominant climate of harmony among a number of key variables, such as teacher and pupil interests; government, local, and school policy; school climate; the demands made on teachers, the resources to meet them, and the rewards to be gained from meeting them; and so on. A potentially stressful situation is set up when a teacher's personal interests, commitment or resources not only get out of line with one or more of the other factors, but actually pull against it. The classic case is having too much work, plus a strong moral imperative to do it, and not enough time and energy within which to do it. A variant on this basic theme is being pressed to do more work, given fewer resources with which to do it, and then receiving no reward or recognition when it is none the less accomplished. An everyday nightmare many teachers face is losing at the last minute a restorative, recharging, idyllic free period and being asked to stand in for an absent colleague with a difficult class. In all of these instances there are elements grating against each other, which compounds the blow to the teacher's sense of well-being. One-off occurrences are to be expected and are probably comparatively easily dealt with. These might cause a 'good row' which clears the air, reminds everybody of the ground rules, is therapeutic to those involved, and hence is functional to the school. Where, on the other hand, there is a degree of permanence behind the underlying causes that produce these fractures, then I would suggest the drain on the teacher's personal resources exceeds their recharge and he/she becomes, gradually perhaps, over time worn down.

Such a model of stress has strong affinities with role conflict. Take, for example, the kind of role conflict arising from conflicting demands from different people. Headteachers are in a highly vulnerable position in this respect. During the troubles of the mid-1980s, for example, they were charged with keeping their schools running by central government, LEAs and parents, yet confronted by the teachers' 'action'. A similar situation arose in the 1960s in a battle over who should do 'dinner duties'. In these power struggles between government, employers and teachers, headteachers have frequently been placed in an impossible position. But to some degree this goes with the job. Standing at the intersection of the school and the outside world, and at the centre of a role-set distinctive for conflicting expectations, they have to be dexterous diplomatists with almost superhuman powers if they are to survive *and* meet the responsibilities of their position.

Deputy headteachers are also in a classically difficult position, being expected to support the head in the running of the school, but also being the spokesperson of the staff. In the not infrequent situation of conflict between a head and the staff, both would expect support. Of course in some respects the seniority of these positions and the status afforded them provides some protection in the form of power and rewards. This does not operate, however, where the conflicts set up on these situations become personalized. I recall a head describing to me the 'traitorous' and 'two-faced' action of her deputy after promising her support over the initiation of a certain policy (unpopular among the staff, but being pushed by the DES and LEA), and then failing to speak up at the crucial staff meeting. 'I'll never forget that', she said, with some venom, 'and I'll never forgive her for it!' This illustrates well how a problem that is basically to do with position and role can be perceived in personal terms, which increases the difficulty and renders it more intractable. Once the conflict invades the private sphere, the role provides little defence.

The teacher role and the production of conflict

Role conflict among senior staff has been further examined by Dunham (1984). Here, I wish to concentrate more on rank-and-file teachers, for, as other chapters in this volume demonstrate, stress is becoming more endemic among them. Even without some of the more obvious recent stress-producing developments (which I shall come to), the teacher role is basically conflictual. Galton (1987), for example, has pointed out that primary school teachers are uncertain about their role in the learning situation. The Plowden Committee (1967) recommended the use of 'informal methods', which, however, can only work in so far as the child can work independently of the teacher. But no guidance is offered on the rules of behaviour within their new situation. Thus teachers tend to take a traditional line with regard to discipline. This may not be particularly stressful in itself, but as the mode of working within primary schools comes to embody a subtle blend of different, and sometimes contradictory elements, so it increases the skill-demand on teachers and puts more of them at risk. Elsewhere (Woods, 1987), I have argued that there is an inherent conflict within the primary school teacher role deriving from the need to combine the functions of teacher (in both instruction and control), parent and friend. To orchestrate these so that there are no discords might be regarded as one of the high points of the teacher's art. But many find it difficult to handle the contradictions involved, like the probationary teacher quoted by Pollard (1985, p. 33) who found it against her nature to be cross with children, though the situation might demand it from time to time:

> I'd rather follow anybody than lead anybody, and to stand up in front of the children and suddenly become this horrible person who had to be nasty to get control . . . it wasn't me in the first place which is why I found it difficult to do.

Such a teacher would stand little chance against pupils like Pollard's (1985, p. 70) 'gang groups' or Beynon's (1985) 'sussers-out'. If the problem is overcome, however, the rewards are great. There is accrued status (Denscombe, 1985) and the satisfaction of overcoming a formidable hurdle.

However, the roots of pupil opposition or non-cooperation run deeper than 'testing' or 'sussing' the teacher out. These lie, some would argue, in the structure of society, in social class, gender and ethnic differences, in socio-economic circumstances, and the way that the educational system is geared towards these, e.g. compulsory education 5–16, the curriculum, and selection (Hargreaves, 1988; Woods, 1988).

For alienated pupils, teachers are the agents of a system that is failing them. In contrast to a previous example where the role afforded protection and difficulty escalated when interpretations shifted to the personal level, the problem here is aggravated the more stringently the role is followed and the more it shifts from the personal. It is susceptible to personal redemption, but it is difficult to keep this up against deep-rooted opposition. A teacher might find that she wins over some recalcitrant pupils one day, only to find she is back where she started the next. The kind of behaviour I have in mind is that of Willis' (1977) 'lads' with their in-built cultural opposition to authority and conformity. Their attitude mirrors those of their parents on the factory shop-floor, and is seen as being similarly related to social structure. Another example is the counter-cultures described by Hargreaves (1988) and Lacey (1977), thrown up in part by the organization of the school into streams (with the counter-culture forming in the lower streams), but also related to social class. Cultures of 'resistance' have been noted among groups of black children who have felt themselves victimized, not only by individual teachers, but by the whole school system (Wright, 1986; Furlong, 1984).

There are several factors involved in this kind of cultural conflict, not least one of different interpretations of the situation by teachers and pupils. Consider this statement from a metalwork teacher in Wright's study (1986, p. 174):

> I had a black girl in my class. She did something or another. I said to her, if you're not careful I'll send you back to the chocolate factory. . . . It was only said in good fun, nothing malicious.

Such a remark might have been 'good fun' for the teacher, but the pupils concerned and their parents clearly thought otherwise. Another teacher was observed to 'pick on' selectively a group of Afro-Caribbean girls and thus to promote confrontation, blaming the girls for her inability to establish conducive learning conditions. In general, black pupils were far more likely than any other group to be placed in ability bands and sets well below their actual academic ability. Cultural opposition was driven further in, and pupils defended themselves by berating a teacher with a stream of Jamaican patois, which of course only confirmed the teacher's fears and sense of opposition. Afro-Caribbean boys also rallied into a strong subcultural group which took a delight in baiting the teachers.

There is a kind of downward spiral here, with teachers and pupils pulling each other further and further under. Teachers often appear to be the villains in these scenarios with their racist taunts and selection injustices. But it is not easy for them. Developing an alternative definition of the situation requires time for reflection, which teachers do not have in great quantity. On the contrary, their working conditions are most alien to self-reflection, and the opportunities for in-service training and sabbaticals are meagre. The pressures and constraints of work either anchor them to current views, attitudes and practices or to very limited reform, and the downward spiral continues.

Are teachers too tied here to official expectations of the role? Why is it so difficult to establish channels of communication? Consider the following testimony from an English teacher who resigned at 28 after only 3½ years teaching (Lock, 1986). At her last school:

> . . . A lot of the staff were scared and apprehensive. One woman teacher spent her lunch hours and breaks hiding in a lavatory. She was really frightened of the kids. She had to do the job – presumably for financial reasons – but she was petrified of it.

She herself had a totally uncooperative class, and 'if you told them off it was you who was in the wrong'. A group of boys in another class:

> were determined to give me a hard time. . . . On one occasion I had hennaed my hair . . . somebody asked in a loud stage whisper, whether I'd had enough left over to do my pubic hair. Then they called me a slag. I thought Christ, I don't need this.

On Fridays she took a class nicknamed 'The Wild Animals'. She remembers on one occasion 'standing there with 20 minutes to go before the bell thinking: Just get in the cupboard and come out in 20 minutes. But I knew I had to stay with them.' Others suffered too:

> A lot of hardened teachers were quietly battling on. They talked about their problems – and the fact that nobody in authority seemed able to do anything to solve them. The teachers were left impotent. There was nothing they could do to make the children work.

Her health suffered, and she began to think 'I was slogging my guts out for next to nothing.' In the end 'the children forced her out'. Now 'when I see schoolkids in the street I think Thank God I got out' (Lock, 1986).

This vividly illustrates the kind of sexual harassment women teachers might be subjected to (see also Walkerdine, 1981; Mahoney, 1985), the feeling of impotence and hopelessness, the physical and emotional investment, and competing definitions of the situation, which includes different expectations of the teacher by the pupil. It was she who was 'in the wrong'. We are familiar with how rules of classroom procedure are 'negotiated' between teacher and pupil (Werthmann, 1963; Rosser and Harre, 1976). In this case, clearly no common ground could be found.

This kind of behaviour by pupils can force teachers to behave in ways inconsistent with their interpretation of the role, even if they are experts at orchestration. Richard Perrins (1986) resigned after 10 years at a London comprehensive. He saw the school 'decay in front of his eyes': 'Some of the buildings had not been decorated for 5 years. Leaks in the roof were not repaired. . . . Chairs and tables were falling to bits and there were never enough of them.' Walls were covered in graffiti, blackboards scored with obscenities, books in hopelessly short supply. This 'decay' sapped the morale and enthusiasm of the staff and pupils alike. Perrins could 'spend long hours preparing lessons – only to find them consumed without appreciation or even interest'. He increasingly came to see 'the secondary school system as a paradigm of society's hierarchical structure . . . a means of teaching people to accept authority without question and know their place in society'. He started to feel less like a teacher, more like a prison warder, alternately conning and bullying his young charges:

> I ended up doing ridiculous things I'd never do outside school – threatening, cajoling, yelling at people. I just didn't want to do it. Finally I realised I was policing a system I no longer believed in.

Disillusioned, underpaid, undervalued, unappreciated, overworked, Perrins resigned shortly after reaching 30 years of age – a notable 'stock-taking' stage of life (see Sikes *et al.*, 1985). He remains committed to education, but not 'within the structures of the existing secondary education system'.

The teacher role and the teacher person

This raises another question. If a teacher is forced to be a police officer, drill-sergeant or welfare officer, to be traditional when progressivism is the aim, or to shout at and be nasty to pupils on occasions when it is not in one's character to do so, what is it doing to the teacher as a person? Here is another source of conflict, therefore, between teacher as teacher, and teacher as person. At the heart of this in many instances is the struggle of the individual with bureaucracy, the problem being to make it work for us with its co-ordination, rules and regulations, its certainty and security; and not against us with its impersonality, hierarchy, resistance to reform, and devotion to extrinsic rewards. Schools and teachers, therefore, have a difficult relationship with bureaucracy. A teacher can become submerged as a person in the role. Blackie (1980), for example, describes how she was seen by her pupils as 'not quite proper'. Asked if they would not be embarrassed to talk about sex with a teacher they knew, during a discussion about sex education, one boy replied: 'Well, yes, maybe, but perhaps we need not have a teacher – perhaps we could have a proper person' (p. 279). On another occasion when they discovered she went to pubs, they were amazed: 'You mean to say . . . you mean . . . that you go to pubs . . . with your friends . . . to pubs . . . just like ordinary people?' (p. 280).

Blackie's school had fewer of the problems of those of Lock's and Perrins'. Teaching was hard work, but enjoyable. However, she was becoming strained through 'the built-in schizophrenia of the job'. This arises from the 'number of different and often explicitly contradictory roles teachers have to fulfil'. Blackie (like Perrin) draws attention to the 'management roles' teachers have to take on 'towards students who do not necessarily choose to be at school, who are not paid to be there, and who are not free to go somewhere else'. Stress arises from the pressure on the person in adjusting between these roles. Blackie does not believe, for example, that she has the right to tell people what clothes to wear. As a teacher, therefore, in a school that has a school uniform, enforcing the rules about it brings on a 'conflict of personal integrity' (p. 281). Teaching involves so much and so frequent role-change, it is no wonder that pupils consider teachers somewhat less than human. Notice, however, the 'double-bind' that teachers are in here, for if they try to break down these barriers, achieve more consistency and appear too human, they will run the risk of being considered 'not proper teachers' (see Woods, 1981).

How a teacher can be submerged under the bureaucracy is illustrated by Bethell (1980), who gave up his head of department post after 10 years because he 'needed a break', 'space to recoup', yet his LEA would not allow him unpaid leave of absence. 'A faint aura of moral disapproval hung over their judgment' (p. 22). Probably they thought that there were sufficient opportunities for secondment. But Bethell points out 'those lucky enough to get seconded have to commit themselves to a course of professional improvement, when what many of them need is a chance for personal enrichment' (p. 23). Looking back he reflects on another stress-inducing feature of teaching:

> As a teacher, and I do not think I was unique in this respect, my every action was tainted by guilt. Not because I did not work hard and not because I was failing, but because however much I did there was always more to be done. I was conditioned, so that the uneasiness would set in at five o'clock on a Sunday afternoon, and not leave hold until the next Saturday morning. Sitting down in front of the television at nine o'clock was always less of an event because of the report I *should* have written, the Chaucer I *should* have prepared, the

teacher I *should* phone or the parent I *should* have contacted. It was not that I had not done enough already; it was merely that the more you did the more there was to do (Bethell, 1980, p. 23).

Such is the character of 'the greedy institution'. It eats you up, always wants more, is never satisfied, the more it consumes the more it needs. One does not have the personal resources for this. Nor are the traditional compensations of bureaucracy in great abundance – the acquisition of status, monetary rewards, career advancement. 'Poor career structure' was, in fact, one of the major sources of stress among Kyriacou and Sutcliffe's (1978) sample, and things have worsened considerably since then (see Roy, 1983 and Ozga, 1988). This is particularly hard on teachers in mid-career. When they first entered the profession in the 1960s, education was undergoing expansion. There were growing opportunities to advance through the Burnham scales and onward to head of department, deputy head and headteacher. When it seemed as if they were losing ground they were given a boost by the Houghton award in 1974. Many of these teachers are now experiencing career-blockage and are having to rethink their career models. Some have been cooled out of the system, through, for example, early retirement. Others have been re-deployed, often a trying, and potentially degrading experience. Many more have worked in the shadow of these trends, and some have themselves found something better than teaching.

This can take a surprising form. Doyle (1987) reports on two technically unemployed sisters, one of whom boosts her income with housework, the other with 'patient-sitting', dog-walking and child-minding. They are both trained teachers with 4–5 years' experience in primary schools:

They make it quite clear that not till hell freezes over would they go back to teaching. They have left behind forever the playground duty, the dinner duty and the endless re-organization and shuffling of timetables due to falling rolls and children in bed and breakfast accommodation for the homeless.

Of course, as Doyle points out, the two sisters might not have been suited to teaching. But a high incidence of such behaviour points away from the individual and towards social factors. This is a point apparently not fully appreciated by the DES and HMI. In a series of reports, such as *The New Teacher in School* (1982), *Teaching Quality* (1983), *Better Schools* (1985a) and *Education Observed 3 – Good Teachers* (1985b), they build up a model of teaching which puts the major emphasis on the personal qualities of teachers. In other words, if teachers were not succeeding, the chances were that there was something deficient in them as teachers. The policy that follows from such a diagnosis is one of repair (for example, by better training), removal of those judged beyond repair, or redeployment to 'suitable' situations. The sense of threat to existing teachers from such an interpretation, especially when coupled with a programme of teacher appraisal, is clear (see Walsh, 1988).

It adds to the menace that it rests on such weak foundations. The reports have been criticized for not making explicit their underlying, pre-existing criteria for 'good teaching'; for not showing how 'personal qualities' arose as a key variable during the research, nor considering how they relate to effective teaching; for categorizing teachers and thus encouraging 'labelling', the counterproductive effects of which have been well demonstrated in respect of pupils (see Hargreaves *et al.*, 1975); for reducing the 'real life' of the classroom to a set of prescriptions (which have their own problems over definition, operationalization and evaluation); and for not giving due weight to other factors that lie beyond the teacher's control (see McNamara, 1986; Broadhead, 1987). Hargreaves (1988) outlines an alternative framework, one that pays due attention to teacher subjectivities and to social factors such as the exigencies of controlling large groups of pupils, situational constraints (such as rooms, furniture, books), examinations, subject specialism, status and career factors, and teacher isolation in their classrooms. Such a model has vastly different policy implications, including the allocation of improved resources to education, weakening of the public examination system, improving systems of staff development and the support of colleagues ('not hierarchical and possibly punitive appraisal'). Hargreaves argues that this would stand a better chance of improving teacher quality. It would certainly reduce teacher stress – perhaps the two are not unconnected.

Survival and non-survival

The DES/HMI model, on the contrary, adds to teachers' problems. The three traditional ways of handling such problems are retreatism (for example, leaving teaching as with some earlier examples), redefinition of the situation (for example, revising one's views of what teaching is about, readjusting one's notion of teaching to a more personally subjective orientation, or updating one's knowledge), and adaptation. With regard to the latter, I have suggested how 'survival strategies' come into being (Woods, 1979). I argue that teachers are subject to a number of pressures and constraints, as already outlined. In recent years these have become more severe. Now there would appear to be two options open to teachers: (i) to try to change the situation, and (ii) to leave it. The first is very difficult, since teachers have little power to influence policy. The second is even more difficult, though apparently on the increase. It is difficult because teachers are committed to their job. They are professionals who tie their energies, loyalties and identities to the system they work in: self, career, achievement and prospects are all identified with the institution. They are highly qualified, and the more they become so, the more committed they become, and the more other options recede. It is a cumulative investment process from which they expect due rewards, not increased pressures. Here we have the classic recipe for stress as defined earlier in this chapter, for these two factors – increased pressures and growing commitment – are on a collision course. Something has to give. It could be their commitment. One might expect, for example, a trend from vocational, professional and total to more instrumental and partial commitment (Sikes *et al.*, 1985). This would not be a complete remedy, for the instrumental prospects have also shrunk, as we have seen. But at least there is less of the self invested in the system, less emotional involvement, less complete dedication to all aspects of the job. The problems thus have less impact.

An alternative, possibly associated course is to adjust one's teaching. I argued in the original research that in that instance it was *teaching* that suffered as teachers were forced into the prior consideration of surviving, and developed a range of 'survival strategies' (such as 'domination', 'fraternization', 'absence', 'therapy').

I am less concerned here with those who survive or do not survive, than with those who are in between, those for whom redefinition or adaptation for some reason or other, is difficult, painful or impossible. Among these, I would suggest, are those teachers who are highly committed, vocationally orientated and 'caring', for there is no escape route open to them. They will not compromise or adulterate their teaching; nor will they change or weaken their commitment. There is nothing left to give way but themselves. The best teachers, arguably, are the most vulnerable. Mike Vernon (1986) was one of these. A successful teacher for 20 years, he suddenly broke down:

It was a Thursday afternoon and I was teaching a fairly bottom-heavy CSE group. I had a good relationship with them and they were behaving no better or worse than they had done before, but you know, there was a constant level of chatter, and one had to work very hard to keep their concentration. I had every confidence in them and I am sure they would have done reasonably well at the end of the course, but I remember thinking to myself 'you can't go on putting in this amount of effort, year after year'. Earlier that afternoon I had taken the sixth form, one of the brightest and nicest I have ever known. They were very demanding and I enjoyed the lesson, but by the end of the day I was in a dreadful state, utterly exhausted. I was in the habit of marking books after tea, but on this occasion I just fell into bed. I awoke about nine o'clock sweating like a pig and trembling. I was in a panic about the marking and started getting the files out, but my wife who is also a teacher, took one look at me and said 'you simply can't go on like this, it's bloody silly'. I think I made a conscious decision then, not to return to teaching (p. 21).

Here, clearly, is a conscientious teacher cracked by the pincer-grip of pressures and commitment. He compares a group of his ex-colleagues who are just as vulnerable as him with teachers who have adjusted their teaching and commitment in the manner discussed above, which he understands but could never countenance himself:

Many of them would like to do what I have done, because they are under stress, but for various reasons they are afraid to leave teaching. I have seen them work day in and day out, year after year with love, and yes, compassion, as the kids come up with one problem after another. It's like parenthood, you can't distance yourself if you are a really caring teacher and want to create a warm and receptive atmosphere.

There has been much debate lately about what teachers should and shouldn't be doing, and implicit in it is the suggestion that they should be in tune with the children, listening to them, and caring about their needs. Yet the way to survive in the present school situation is the reverse. Many teachers build great walls of defence around themselves, teaching subjects in a cold and formal way, year after year, and distancing themselves from the children. They 'survive' and one is tempted to admire them in an awful twisted sort of way. But the thought of becoming like them brings you to your senses. There is no doubt at all that it is the caring teacher who is most vulnerable to stress (p. 21).

Vernon receives an invalidity pension, and while he feels 'fortunate' in some respects, he is concerned that some people will consider him 'inefficient' because he dropped out, thus re-emphasizing the psychological pressure that keeps many others similar to him grinding away at the job. He concludes:

I feel desperately angry that society and the Government don't understand what the present demands are doing to teachers. I want my children to go to a school where the teachers are fairly happy and ready to work and where they are not under exceptional stress and have the time and resources to do the job properly (p. 21).

Conclusion

I have argued that stress arises when elements grate against each other and thus produce a special kind of difficulty which puts an excessive strain on a teacher's personal resources. These elements on their own and when not related together in direct opposition are handled with more equanimity. This is not to say they are easily dealt with, for teaching is a demanding job at the best of times.

From this point of view the teacher role is a potential source of considerable stress, for it produces conflicts of such a nature. There are conflicts caused by different people's different expectations of the teacher (for example, where the pupils considered the teacher to be 'in the wrong'), there are within-role conflicts (for example, between teacher as instructor/controller and teacher as parent/friend), and conflicts set up by tension between the person and the role (such as experienced by the teacher who felt the need of 'personal enrichment' rather than 'professional enhancement'). The ones most at risk here would seem to be:

1 Probationary and inexperienced teachers, for they have not yet learned how to cope with the dilemmas and contradictions.
2 Teachers who lack knowledge and understanding, perhaps through no fault of their own, of such things as pupil cultures (some of these matters are not well understood by anybody, and teachers are given little time for reflection and/or in-service training (see also Dunham, 1984).
3 Teachers who find it difficult, for whatever reason, to 'orchestrate' their teaching.
4 Senior teachers, such as heads and deputies, who are in the position of greatest role conflict.

There is, in addition, another group of teachers for whom circumstances and recent developments have made the management of role conflict and satisfactory role performance exceptionally difficult. These include:

1 Career-aspiring teachers, especially those in mid-career, who face career blockage, for they lose the main reward that helps balance out the increased pressures, and experience instead profound frustration.
2 The caring and highly committed teachers who refuse to compromise their high ideals, and who are faced with increased physical and emotional strain on the one hand and less self-fulfilling performance of the role with less investment of the self on the other.

Personal qualities must come into consideration somewhere, but only, I would argue, as a local factor. One teacher might manage better than another in a given situation, all other things being equal. However, the growing incidence of stress across the profession as demonstrated in other chapters in this volume points strongly to other factors, which, I have suggested, aggravate the teacher's perennial problem of role conflict. There is no doubt that many teachers are experiencing serious problems, and that the morale of the profession as a whole is low – a contributory factor to stress in itself (Coverdale, 1973). The root cause of all this, I would argue, lies mainly outside the schools and is to do with the kind of educational system envisaged and how it is resourced.

Having said this, it must be acknowledged that there are many successful, and indeed content, teachers. This is testimony to their ingenuity and dedication, to their ability to use the role for their purposes, and/or to find alternative career patterns within teaching; to many schools for developing climates that are supportive of their staff; to LEAs, heads and deputies who work constructively and creatively together and with their staffs. They are coping, as most teachers will. This should not blind us to those who are having to battle to make a success of the job with inadequate resources, and the consequent very real threat to the general efficiency of the system.

References

Berlack, A. and Berlack, H. (1981). *The Dilemmas of Schooling*. Methuen: London.

Bethell, A. (1980). Getting away from it all. *Times Educational Supplement* 21 March, 22–3.

Beynon, J. (1985). *Initial Encounters in the Secondary School*. Falmer Press: Lewes, Sussex.

Blackie, P. (1980). Not quite proper. In Reedy, S. and Woodhead, M. (eds), *Family, Work and Education*. Hodder and Stoughton: London.

Broadhead, P. (1987). A blueprint for the good teacher? The HMI/DES model of good primary practice. *British Journal of Educational Studies* **xxxv**(1), 57–72.

Coverdale, G. M. (1973). Some determinants of teacher morale. *Educational Review* **26**(1), 30–8.

Denscombe, M. (1985). *Classroom Control: A Sociological Perspective*. Allen and Unwin: London.

Department of Education and Science (1982). *The New Teacher in School*. HMSO: London.

Department of Education and Science (1983). *Teaching Quality*. HMSO: London.

Department of Education and Science (1985a). *Better Schools*. HMSO: London.

Department of Education and Science (1985b). *Education Observed 3 – Good Teachers*. HMSO: London.

Doyle, V. (1987). When school is very definitely out. *Guardian* 11 August.

Dunham, J. (1984). *Stress in Teaching*. Croom Helm: London.

Furlong, V. J. (1984). Black resistance in the liberal comprehensive. In Delamont, S. (ed.), *Readings on Interaction in the Classroom*. Methuen: London.

Galton, M. (1987). An ORACLE chronicle: a decade of classroom research. In Delamont, S. (ed.), *The Primary School Teacher*. Falmer Press: Lewes.

Grace, G. (1972). *Role Conflict and the Teacher*. Routledge and Kegan Paul: London.

Hargreaves, A. (1988). Teaching quality: A sociological analysis. *Journal of Curriculum Studies*, forthcoming.

Hargreaves, D. H., Hester, S. K. and Mellor, F. J. (1975). *Deviance in Classrooms.* Routledge and Kegan Paul: London.

Kyriacou, C. (1987). Teacher stress and burnout: An international review. *Educational Research* **29**(2), 146–52.

Kyriacou, C. and Sutcliffe, J. (1978). Teacher stress and satisfaction. *Educational Research* **21**(2), 89–109.

Lacey, C. (1977). *The Socialization of Teachers.* Methuen: London.

Lock, L. (1986). In Godfrey, M., Telling tales out of school. *Guardian* 12 March, 22.

Mahoney, P. (1985). *Schools for the Boys.* Hutchinson: London.

McNamara, D. (1986). The personal qualities of the teacher and educational policy: a critique. *British Educational Research Journal* **12**(1), 29–36.

Ozga, J. (1988). Teachers' Work and Careers, Unit W1 of Course EP228. *Frameworks for Teaching.* Open University Press: Milton Keynes.

Perrins, R. (1986). In Godfrey, M., Telling tales out of school. *Guardian* 12 March, 22.

Plowden Report (1967). *Children and their Primary Schools.* Report of the Central Advisory Council for Education in England. HMSO: London.

Pollard, A. (1985). *The Social World of the Primary School.* Holt, Rinehart and Winston: London.

Rosser, E. and Harre, R. (1976). The meaning of disorder. In Hammersley, M. and Woods, P. (eds), *The Process of Schooling,* Routledge and Kegan Paul: London.

Roy, W. (1983). *Teaching Under Attack.* Croom Helm: London.

Sikes, P., Measor, L. and Woods, P. (1985). *Teacher Careers: Crises and Continuities.* Falmer Press: Lewes, Sussex.

Vernon, M. (1986). A burnt out case. *Times Educational Supplement* 31 January.

Walkerdine, V. (1981). Sex, power and pedagogy. *Screen Education* **38**, 14–24.

Waller, W. (1932). *The Sociology of Teaching.* John Wiley: New York.

Walsh, K. (1988). Appraising the teachers: Professionalism and control. In Dale, R., Fergusson, R. and Robinson, A. (eds), *Frameworks for Teaching: Readings for the Intending Secondary Teacher.* Hodder and Stoughton: London.

Werthmann, C. (1963). Delinquents in school: A test for the legitimacy of authority. *Berkeley Journal of Sociology* **8**(i), 39–60.

Willis, P. (1977). *Learning to Labour.* Saxon House: Farnborough.

Woods, P. (1979). *The Divided School.* Routledge and Kegan Paul: London.

Woods, P. (1981). Strategies, commitment and identity: Making and breaking the teacher role. In Barton, L. and Walker, S. (eds), *Schools, Teachers and Teaching.* Falmer Press: Lewes, Sussex.

Woods, P. (1987). The management of the primary school teacher's role. In Delamont, S. (ed.), *The Primary School Teacher.* Falmer Press: Lewes.

Woods, P. (1988). The Quality of Teaching, Unit 12 of Course E208. *Exploring Educational Issues.* Open University Press: Milton Keynes.

Wright, C. (1986). School processes – an ethnographic study. In Eggleston, J., Dunn, D. and Anjali, M. (eds), *Education for Some: the Educational and Vocational Experiences of 15–18 Year Old Members of Minority Ethnic Groups.* Trentham Books: Stoke-on-Trent.

5 CONTAINING STRESS

Comment: Who cares?

The association of teaching with stress is not new. As long ago as 1932, Willard Waller, with characteristic bluntness observed:

> *The lunatic fringe of teaching, every year sloughed off and every year renewed, is made of personalities battered by many trauma.*

Waller did not mean to be unkind to teachers. Indeed, inspired by what can only be regarded as a Freudian fervour, he went on to suggest that a real way of giving teachers positive support would be to analyse their dreams (and nightmares) so as to reveal sources of tension and professional stress:

> *The dreams of teachers . . . show where the points of stress and strain appear in the school situation as it affects the teacher.*

And the examples he gives are pretty horrific. But, psychoanalysis apart, Waller's basic observation does raise some interesting and important questions. Who is responsible for monitoring and managing the mental health of teachers and how should that responsibility be met? As stress in teaching has become more noticeable and has been taken more seriously, one kind of answer to these questions has been the deployment of 'professional stress managers', people brought in from outside of a school, or even teaching, so as to develop courses and programmes aimed at increasing teacher awareness and reducing teacher anxiety. Although most of these initiatives have been well-intentioned, the previous lack of any systematic provision for teachers' occupational health has meant that many of them have been based on knowledge and attitudes developed in other work settings, in non-teaching situations. As a consequence, many of these training schemes have not had access to analytical models and insights which are specifically sensitive to those organizational and institutional sources of stress which are quite peculiar to schools or to teaching.

The paper by Cox et al., which follows, stands as a corrective to this tradition.

The approach these writers take is grounded in action. To this end, they explore ways of developing a model of teaching and stress in which teachers themselves, armed with the insights available from stress research done in non-teaching environments, are empowered to generate their own analyses, explanations and coping strategies. In this way, teachers take responsibility themselves for the identification and alleviation of stress in their work; stress research in action – and action in stress research.

Reference

Waller, W. (1932). *The Sociology of Teaching.* John Wiley: New York.

STRESS IN SCHOOLS: A PROBLEM-SOLVING APPROACH*

Tom Cox, Neil Boot and Sue Cox

Overview

During the last 25 years there has been increasing professional and public interest in issues relating to occupational stress and health, and during the late 1960s this interest began to focus on those employed within the service sector, particularly on those involved in education, health and welfare. At that time, the question was posed 'who cares for the carers?', and since then occupational psychologists and other related groups have been proving their interest by attempting to describe the problems faced by such staff and the effects of those problems on both their well-being and performance.

Teachers have been a popular target for such research, and from the late 1970s onwards there have been many English language publications concerned with studies on teachers, and from many different countries, including, e.g. the UK (Cox, 1977; Cox and Brockley, 1984; Dewe, 1985; Dunham, 1984; Fimian, 1984; Kyriacou, 1980; Kyriacou and Pratt, 1985;

---

* The authors wish to thank the various Authorities and other institutions that have supported their current work, and that have offered funding to support further research. The views presented here are those of the authors and do not necessarily reflect those of any other person or any organization.

Kyriacou and Sutcliffe, 1977; Payne and Fletcher, 1983; Pont and Reid, 1985; Pratt, 1978), the USA (Farber, 1984; MacIntyre, 1984), Canada (Hiebert and Farber, 1984), Israel (Kremer and Hofman, 1985; Smilansky, 1984), Sweden (Tellenback *et al.*, 1983) and Australia (Docking, 1985; Laughlin, 1984). Generally, it was agreed during the early years that 'job related stress in teachers is a growing problem' (ILO, 1981) and that 'more teachers are now experiencing stress than ever before' (Dunham, 1975).

Studies on occupational stress and health in the service sector, like those cited above, are of academic interest for two reasons (Johansson, 1987). First, our general understanding of the nature and effects of occupational stress has been very much built up on studies in the primary (extractive) and secondary (manufacturing) sectors. Unfortunately, it cannot be assumed that models derived from these studies will generalize to the tertiary (service) sector. Secondly, and related to the first point, the majority of those working and studied in the primary and secondary sectors were men, while many of those working in the tertiary sector are women (see, e.g. Cox *et al.*, 1984). Our ability to understand the latter in terms of the former must be challenged. Both these points must be taken into account when interpreting studies on stress in schools in the wider context of occupational stress and health. Thus studies on teachers could break new theoretical ground if compared to earlier studies outside the tertiary sector.

However, while possibly breaking new ground in these respects, such studies on stress in schools have generally failed to develop past the established paradigm of considering the teacher's experience in isolation from their organizational context. This is somewhat surprising as, at the same time, many studies report that the problems faced by teachers are organizational (or managerial) in origin (see p. 106).

At the same time, many studies have only considered an analysis of the problems faced by teachers, and have not systematically considered the different strategies available for their solution. Those that have, have often made very general recommendations focused on the individual teacher – relaxation training, access to a counsellor, use of tranquillizers, etc. Sadly, these individually orientated 'band aids' have further detracted from the important role that the organization plays in determining teachers' experiences. Equally, neglecting this organizational perspective has led to a failure to ask and answer questions about the health and performance of the organization itself, or about organizational solutions to these problems.

This chapter considers 'stress in schools' in the context of a programme of work currently being carried out by the authors, which was initially designed to promote an organizational view of the issue of stress in schools, and to deliberately explore organizational and managerial strategies for dealing with that problem.

PROBLEM-SOLVING APPROACH

It was agreed at the outset that the approach to be followed in this work was to be based on 'real world' problem solving, set within the context of general systems theory (Checkland, 1972). This genre of approach has been discussed in relation to research into stress in nurses (Hingley and Cooper, 1986) and in relation to personal coping (Cox, 1987). Such an approach dictated that:

1 The school as an organization has to be thought of in terms of both its structure, and the processes which support its function, and that this model be set in its wider context (or environment), and that account is taken of its general climate or culture. This analysis has to be 'top down' from the highest level to the lowest sensible level which maintains some recognizable integrity of activity on the part of individual teachers.

2 Such an analysis is the essential first step in addressing the issue of the practical management of stress in schools through what is essentially a four-stage process: analysis, selection of action strategies, implementation and evaluation.

The information required for the first two stages, analysis and selection of action strategies, may be collected in a variety of ways. In the present project, and for a variety of practical reasons, it was decided that 'exploratory workshops' would afford a suitable method of data capture, which would marry research and development objectives with training:

3 Following the paradigm implicit in the problem-solving approach (as applied to stress-related phenomena; Cox, 1987), it was decided that the analysis of such problems should be set within a declared theoretical framework, and this was provided by the senior author's transactional approach to occupational stress (Cox, 1978, 1985; Cox and Mackay, 1981). This describes stressful scenarios in terms of four factors: (i) the demands and pressures of the person or persons involved, (ii) their personal coping resources (and how well matched they are to those demands and pressures), (iii) the control that those people have over the work that they do (or conversely the constraints that are imposed on their coping) and, finally, (iv) the support available to them from others both within and outside the work situation.

4 It was also decided that problem solving within the present context should be based on a 'participative approach' with considerable control over the nature and speed of 'progress' being invested in the teacher groups involved, while maintaining the overall project objectives.

These essentially methodological issues were explained to and discussed with those teachers who became involved in the various aspects of the project, and were also incorporated into the different expert inputs to the project's workshops.

The project

An opportunity to pursue this plan was afforded during late 1986. Following a prolonged period of industrial dispute within the British education system, which affected most if not all schools in the public sector, there was a felt need to promote not only the well-being of individual teachers but also that of schools as organizations. Following an approach by an education authority in the East Midlands, interested in 'stress management training' for its senior teachers, the present project 'came to life'. It is described below in terms of four phases. The first two phases concern the original authority, the third phase involves a second authority, in the south of the Midland region, while the fourth phase is just beginning with further research into stress in schools funded by several different organizations.

FIRST PHASE: EAST MIDLAND WORKSHOPS

Contact with the original authority was established through their Secondary Schools Advisor, who was interested in exploring the possible usefulness of 'stress management training' for middle and senior teachers within the authority's schools. During a series of discussions, a number of important points of agreement emerged:

1 That there was a shared concern that the school and not the individual teacher should be the focus of any 'stress management' initiative.
2 That simply educating managers was necessary but not sufficient to produce change within schools.
3 That decisions on what else might be done, where, how and when should involve those managers and other teachers within the schools.
4 That while the phrase 'stress in schools' was sufficiently 'attractive' to arouse general interest in the project, it was too threatening a banner under which to develop later specific initiatives within schools.

After further discussions, it was agreed that a series of four workshops would be carried out for that authority's senior school management; one in each of their education areas. Representative samples of schools in each area were approached by the Secondary School Advisor and up to two teachers were invited to attend from each school. The Advisor explained the nature and objectives of the workshop to the senior teachers in each school. The workshops were treated as training days. Each workshop had between 12 and 14 participants, each of which was an informed volunteer.

Content

The 'stress management' workshops were designed according to three principles:

1 They would involve 'process' as well as 'knowledge'; they would give the teachers skills that could be applied to the management of school life as well as increasing their general awareness.
2 They would be interactive, and that participants would be given the opportunity to use the ideas and practise the skills introduced during the day.
3 They would focus on the management and organizational aspects of stress in schools, treating the school as one unit of analysis.

There were two 'expert' briefings in each workshop. The first described the nature and analysis of stressful situations at work, and was based on the theoretical position developed by the senior author and described above (Cox, 1978, 1985; Cox and Mackay, 1981). This was supported by syndicate work mapping and analysing problems identified within schools, or presented using a series of case studies (on video). The second briefing was a review of current practice with regards to the management of stress within organizations (Cox, 1988), and was supported by an exploratory planning exercise.

Feedback

Information from each of the syndicate exercises was collected by the expert team during each workshop, and fed forward to the next. At the end of the series, the information was collated and reported back to the authority through their Senior Schools Advisor. This information is discussed below.

Evaluation

As a necessary and planned part of the overall strategy (see Checkland, 1972; Cox, 1987), the Advisor was asked to organize a separate evaluation of the workshops. Unfortunately, the design of this evaluation exercise was, by force of circumstance, somewhat inadequate, in that it was based on a single enquiry to the participant group only. It appeared that, for political reasons, it was not possible to use a more elaborate design. The workshops were held during the last months of the teachers' dispute.

The evaluation posed a number of different questions about the workshops, and the information gained was generally both supportive and informative. Of particular interest here is the question: 'Did the workshop meet your expectations?' The response to this question was captured on a 10-point scale (from 0 'not at all' through 5 'completely up to expectations' to 10 'exceeded expectations'). Of the 17 teachers who replied to this question, 16 (94 per cent) said that it completely met or exceeded their expectations. A similar proportion reported that the information and 'skills' that they had gained during the day were proving useful in their school situation.

Generally, the teachers responding to the evaluation asked that the issue be kept at the front of the professional debate, and that the present project be supported as part of a broad attack on stress in schools. They also asked that guidelines be developed for senior teachers, and that action be taken to develop better support networks within their authority.

SECOND PHASE: DEVELOPMENT OF A MODEL FOR FOLLOWING THROUGH

Following the positive evaluation of the workshops by the senior teachers involved, the Advisor called a meeting of key 'heads of schools' in her authority, and at that meeting the expert team explored their suggestions for the way forward. A model emerged from that meeting which comprised two related strategies:

1 A continuation of the workshops, extending to middle as well as senior school managers, with the aim of training a critical mass of teachers within the authority.
2 The provision of the expert team as a resource for individual schools to assist them in any further actions they wish to take in relation to stress in schools.

It was also suggested that, subject to the availability of appropriate funds, the education authority would support the former strategy, whereas individual schools would support the latter out of their own finances.

Unfortunately, due to changes at authority level, the continuation of the workshop programme has been delayed, although still subject to negotiations. However, the first steps have been taken at school level (second strategy): two schools have expressed an interest in developing their own action programmes, and are now consulting with the team.

THIRD AND FOURTH PHASES: MORE WORKSHOPS AND FURTHER RESEARCH

A second education authority, in the south of the Midland region, has now joined the project, and a series of workshops based on the design, methods and objectives described above, are now being conducted for their senior teachers. In order to provide good local support for this second initiative, the authority's educational psychologists have also been trained in the theory and processes underpinning the workshops and the workshop methods. This Department will eventually take over the project, providing support for individual schools, but in continued consultation with the expert team.

Finally, because of their interest in the workshop project, financial support for further research into stress in schools has been made available by one of the teacher Unions and by a concerned organization in the banking, insurance and finance sector.

Analysis: The nature of stress in schools

Information relevant to the analysis of the problem of stress in schools was collected from the senior teachers attending the first series of workshops (East Midlands). It is discussed below in the context of other relevant studies.

An industrial study was carried out by the Stress Research Group during the late 1970s which examined the different sources of stress reported by men and women working in four East Midland companies (Cox *et al.*, 1981). All four companies were in the manufacturing sector, and the respondents were drawn at random from a stratified sample of both manual and non-manual (ancillary, managerial and clerical) workers. Among other things, the study posed a relatively simple and direct question concerning the source of any stress they were currently experiencing. Four different domains were covered in their responses: work (53.7 per cent), work–home interface (11.9 per cent), home (20.9 per cent) and others (13.4 per cent) including financial, physical and social problems. Work, not surprisingly, was the major problem domain for most questioned. In a separate community-based survey, also carried out in the East Midlands (Cox *et al.*, 1981), the sources of stress reported by a sample of teachers were somewhat similarly examined and compared to those reported by a sample of non-teachers matched for age, sex and socio-economic status. This study revealed that significantly more teachers reported experiencing stress than did non-teachers, and that more teachers reported work as a source of stress than did non-teachers.

Another study, conducted by the author and his colleagues at this time (Cox, 1977; Brockley, 1978; Cox and Brockley, 1984) extended these findings. Initially a mixed group of teachers (drawn from two education authorities in North Wales) were asked to identify the 10 most dissatisfying and the 10 most satisfying aspects of their work. These data were used to contrast sources of satisfaction and dissatisfaction, and to compare their relative importance, but they also afforded a preliminary structuring of the then reported sources of stress. At that time there appeared to be five major groups of stressful situations:

- training and career development;
- the nature of work (classroom situation, pupil behaviour, workload, resources and teaching methods);
- the physical work environment;
- the school organization (size of school, school management, role of the teacher and communication); and
- the relationship between the school and community.

Subsequent work by Brockley (1978) attempted to relate a measure of dissatisfaction based on this classification to teachers' self-reported health. His data showed that the total number of symptoms reported during a 6-month time window was significantly related to a measure of pupil (mis)behaviour but not to the other sources of stress identified. The classroom situation was therefore 'flagged', at that time, as being of particular importance with respect to stress in schools. This was consistent with the findings of some other researchers (e.g. Galloway *et al.*, 1982; Laslett and Smith, 1984) but not all (see Kyriacou, 1987). Interestingly, in his recent review of teacher stress and burnout, Kyriacou (1987) concludes:

It is surprising to find that pupils' poor attitudes to work, and too heavy a workload, have been generally found to be the main sources of stress, and not disruptive behaviour by pupils *per se*.

On the basis of our early data, and indeed our later data too, it would be difficult to agree with this statement as it stands. Although the factors identified by Kyriacou (1987) are obviously important sources of stress for many teachers they were not cited as the *most* important. Furthermore, Kyriacou (1987) fails to discuss the impact of the organization and its management on teachers' problems in schools. Perhaps the source of this discrepancy lies in the nature of the samples studied: in our studies, the perceptions of senior teachers have been sought, whereas this has not been so in most other studies.

Nearly 10 years on, the feedback from the first series of workshops (East Midlands) painted a somewhat similar picture, although with some new elements having been introduced. Five different domains were reported as sources of stress for teachers within the school organization:

- those stemming from training and career development;
- those inherent in the job;

- those reflecting the personal characteristics of certain teachers;
- those relating to the school organization, management and culture; and
- those external to the school related to political and community expectations.

Without providing a detailed discussion of all the points and issues raised, it is worth noting three of particular interest. First, teachers' concern for problems inherent in the job focused on the classroom situation. They variously reported difficulties arising from being continually exposed to the pupil population (and one which was not necessarily motivated to learn and was occasionally hostile), feeling isolated in the classroom and unsure as to the education authority's position on disruptive pupils. Secondly, the school was thought to offer a poor problem-solving environment; one in which problems were cast as individual rather than team concerns. There was reported to be little team spirit, a lack of formal problem-solving channels and a lack of shared standards, values and aims. The school was not seen as a supportive work environment. Thirdly, there was seen to be a major issue related to 'change'; not only the fact of change, but change-on-change, beyond the control of most teachers. There was no felt involvement in the change process and no sense of ownership of what was happening. Change was being imposed from 'elsewhere'.

The impression built up from this feedback was one in which not only were individual teachers experiencing stress through various aspects of their work, but also that schools as organizations were not themselves in a healthy state.

Selection of action strategies: Stress management in schools

Managing stress at work is a relatively new area of concern, and one which brings together two rather different disciplines: organizational psychology and occupational health.

Essentially, stress management programmes share one of three objectives (Cox, 1988):

1 To prevent the occurrence of stressful situations at work, or to reduce the frequency with which they occur.
2 To increase awareness of such problems, so that they can be more easily and rapidly picked up, and to improve the problem-solving strategies with which they are then dealt with.
3 To treat or rehabilitate individuals (and organizations) who have experienced stress.

Briefly, the various possible strategies, derived to meet these objectives, are mirrored in three questions posed in the spirit of the Health and Safety at Work Act, 1974:

- what can the organization do to put its own house in order;
- what can the organization do to help or assist its employees; and
- what can those employees do to help themselves?

WHAT CAN THE ORGANIZATION DO FOR ITSELF?

Stressful situations may arise because of failures of selection or initial training, or of up-dating staff. They may arise because jobs, technology or work environments have not been designed with staff in mind. They might arise because of the management style and practice, or because of the very nature and culture of the organization. Thus there are several different ways in which the organization can put its house in order. None are magical, mystical or particularly new: they involve a careful consideration of (a) the organization's structure, function and culture, (b) the nature of its line management, and (c) the effectiveness of its specialist management.

WHAT CAN THE ORGANIZATION DO FOR ITS STAFF?

In addition to taking a long, hard and possibly critical look at itself, the organization can also consider what else can be provided for its staff.

A relatively small number of large organizations support a traditional occupational health service, rather more buy into one of this country's private medical services, such as BUPA Occupational Health. In addition, many organizations, both in the USA and in Europe, also offer their staff access to special programmes designed to improve their general health and fitness, and help them cope with the challenge of work. These programmes have been given a whole variety of different titles, but are perhaps most easily recognized as 'employee assistance' or 'employee health' programmes. Our evidence suggests that such programmes have several common elements: the provision of health promotion information (usually smoking cessation, weight control, controlled drinking and diet), fitness and relaxation training, group discussions and/or access to a professional counsellor or, better still, a personal consultant psychologist, and training in coping skills (such as time management or assertiveness).

Although set up and sponsored by the organization, these programmes can only succeed if the individuals involved are convinced of their value and are drawn into participation. They have to accept at least part-ownership of their problems. Much of what is on offer can be taken on board by those individuals outside of work, perhaps as part of developing a healthier and more robust lifestyle. Thus the question 'what can the organization do for individuals' becomes 'what can the individuals do for themselves?' There are several different ways in which individuals can improve their well-being and ability to meet the challenge of work.

WHAT CAN INDIVIDUALS DO FOR THEMSELVES?

There seem to be three areas in which the person can improve their lifestyle and promote fitness in the face of challenging demands:

- the behavioural domain (better intake and energy management);
- the psychological domain (improved time management, improved management of emotion, and better problem-solving skills); and
- the social domain (actively developing social support networks).

Sadly, there is only a little evidence currently available on the relative effectiveness of any of these different stress management strategies. This is one reason why the European Stress Management Programme has been established at Nottingham University. Working in conjunction with groups such as the Centre for Extension Studies at Loughborough University and Maxwell and Cox Associates, it is attempting to identify, describe and evaluate such programmes and activities. Together the intention is to build up a database on their relative successes and failures, and examine critically the processes underpinning each.

The senior teachers involved in the first series of workshops (East Midlands) made many interesting suggestions for possible actions relating to the management of stress in schools. Reflecting the nature of the project these mainly focused on managerial and organizational actions:

- team problem solving,
- positive management of change,
- development of staff health and recreational facilities,
- provision of an integrated (long-term) staff development programme, involving provision for time management skills, and
- deliberate development of the social climate and social support within schools.

Overall, it was felt by these teachers that there was a need to 'draw the discussion of stress out of the closet' and make it a legitimate part of the school debate.

Two general objectives loomed large in the comments made. First, there was a need to develop a more cooperative and supportive culture within schools, and to manage positively a team approach to problem solving. To do this, group problem solving would need to be legitimized and time would have to be made available for this process. Secondly, the rate of change should be slowed down, and senior teachers, in conjunction with the education authority, should consider how this might be best done to give teachers time to adapt. However, perhaps more important, was a recognition of the need to involve teachers in the change process as soon and as much as possible. Steps had to be taken to encourage ownership of change, and a more positive attitude to it. Thirdly, it was recognized that while there were nursing, medical and recreational facilities available for pupils in schools, and even the wider community, through schools, little was made available to the teachers, despite the necessary expertise which existed within most schools. Three specific suggestions were made:

1 An employee health service, encompassing health promotion programmes should be provided for staff.
2 An independent counselling service should be established for staff.
3 Leisure and exercise facilities and courses should be developed for them.

In other discussions of how schools might tackle stress-related problems (e.g. Fletcher and Payne, 1982; Dunham, 1984; Kyriacou, 1981) the most frequently advocated changes relate to:

1 The nature of the job (clearer job descriptions, giving teachers more preparation time during the school day and reducing the size of classes).
2 Improved school organization, communication and climate.
3 More effective staff induction and development programmes.
4 Greater recognition of teachers' efforts, and a clearer description of the expectations placed on them.

These obviously relate to the various sources of stress described above from the Nottingham-based studies (see pp. 102–105). They differ slightly from the action strategies described in this section, possibly because they were, by and large, not derived from senior school management. However, it can be readily seen that they are conceptually consistent with the senior teachers' suggestions.

Implementation and evaluation

The next step is obviously to examine these and other proposals in more detail and establish their feasibility before planning their implementation. This process is now beginning in two ways: through the feedback of such information to the education authorities involved, and by feed forward to other workshops for further discussion with teachers. At the same time, the question of evaluation is being raised.

Summary

Over the past 15 or so years, there has been much research into the nature of stress in schools which has allowed an analysis of this problem, although mainly from the perspective of the individual teacher. More recent studies, particularly through the Nottingham-based team, have added an organizational dimension to this analysis, and have provided the initial steps in selecting suitable action strategies for dealing with those problems. The Nottingham project is firmly based in a problem-solving approach to stress in schools, set very much within a framework provided by general systems theory.

References

Brockley, T. (1978). The nature and incidence of occupational stress among Gwynedd school teachers. Unpublished M.Ed. thesis, University College of North Wales, Bangor.

Checkland, P. B. (1972). Towards a systems based methodology for real world problem solving. *Journal of Systems Engineering* **3**, 2.

Cox, T. (1977). *The Nature and Management of Stress in Schools*. Education Department, Clwyd County Council: Mold.

Cox, T. (1978). *Stress*. Macmillan: London.

Cox, T. (1985). The nature and measurement of stress. *Ergonomics* **28**, 1155–63.

Cox, T. (1987). Stress, coping and problem solving. *Work and Stress* **1**, 5–14.

Cox, T. (1988). Stress in organizations: Meeting the challenge of work. BUPA Symposium: *The Management of Health*. Sheraton, Edinburgh (March).

Cox, T. and Brockley, T. (1984). The experience and effects of stress in teachers. *British Journal of Educational Research* **10**, 83–7.

Cox, T. and Mackay, C. J. (1981). A transactional approach to occupational stress. In Corlett, N. and Richardson, J. (eds), *Stress, Work Design and Productivity*. John Wiley: Chichester.

Cox, T., Watts, C. and Barnett, C. A. (1981). The experience and effects of task inherent demand. Report to US Army Research Institute (European Office). Stress Research Group, Department of Psychology, University of Nottingham, Nottingham.

Cox, T., Cox, S. and Steventon, J. (1984). Women at work: Summary and overview. *Ergonomics* **27**, 597–605.

Dewe, P. (1985). Coping with work stress: An investigation of teachers' action. *Research in Education* **33**, 27–40.

Docking, R. A. (1985). Changing teacher–pupil control ideology and teacher anxiety. *Journal of Education for Teaching* **11**, 63–76.

Dunham, J. (1975). Re-organisation and stress: Apprehensive and vulnerable teachers. *Journal of Applied Education Studies* **4**, 34–9.

Dunham, J. (1984). *Stress in Teaching*. Croom Helm: London.

Farber, B. A. (1984). Stress and burn out in suburban teachers. *Journal of Educational Research* **77**, 325–31.

Fimian, M. J. (1984). The development of an instrument to measure occupational stress in teachers: The Teacher Stress Inventory. *Journal of Occupational Psychology* **57**, 277–93.

Fletcher, B. C. and Payne, R. L. (1982). Levels of reported stressors and strains amongst school teachers: Some UK data. *Educational Review* **34**, 267–78.

Galloway, D., Ball, T., Blomfield, D. and Seyd, R. (1982). *Schools and Disruptive Pupils*. Longman: London.

Hiebert, B. and Farber, I. (1984). Teacher stress: A literature survey with a few surprises. *Canadian Journal of Education* **9**, 14–27.

Hingley, P. and Cooper, C. L. (1986). *Stress and the Nurse Manager*. John Wiley: Chichester.

International Labour Office (1981). *Employment and Conditions of Work of Teachers*. International Labour Office: Geneva.

Johansson, G. (1987). Invisible gender. *Work and Stress* **1**, 324.

Kremer, L. and Hofman, J. E. (1985). Teachers: Professional identity and burn out. *Research in Education* **34**, 89–95.

Kyriacou, C. (1980). Coping actions and occupational stress among teachers. *Research in Education* **24**, 57–61.

Kyriacou, C. (1981). Social support and occupational stress among school teachers. *Educational Studies* **7**, 55–60.

Kyriacou, C. (1987). Teacher stress and burnout: An international review. *Educational Research* **29**, 146–52.

Kyriacou, C. and Pratt, J. (1985). Teacher stress and psychoneurotic symptoms. *British Journal of Educational Psychology* **55**, 61–4.

Kyriacou, C. and Sutcliffe, J. (1977). Teacher stress: A review. *Educational Review* **29**, 299–306.

Laslett, R. and Smith, C. (1984). *Effective Classroom Management*. Croom Helm: London.

Laughlin, A. (1984). Teacher stress in an Australian setting: The role of biographical mediators. *Educational Studies* **10**, 7–22.

MacIntyre, T. C. (1984). The relationship between locus of control and teacher burn out. *British Journal of Educational Psychology* **54**, 235–8.

Payne, R. L. and Fletcher, B.C. (1983). Job demands, supports and constraints as predictors of psychological strain among school teachers. *Journal of Vocational Behaviour* **22**, 136–47.

Pont, H. and Reid, G. (1985). Stress and special education: The need for transactional data. *Scottish Educational Review* **17**, 107–15.

Pratt, J. (1978). Perceived stress among teachers: The effects of age and background of children taught. *Educational Review* **30**, 3–14.

Smilansky, J. (1984). External and internal correlates of teachers' satisfaction and willingness to report stress. *British Journal of Educational Psychology*, **54**, 84–92.

Tellenback, S., Brenner, S.-O. and Lofgren, H. (1983). Teacher stress: Exploratory model building. *Journal of Occupational Psychology* **56**, 19–33.

PART 2

TACKLING STRESS IN TEACHING

6 COPING STRATEGIES

Comment: Take a deep breath . . .

Inevitably, increased evidence and increased interest in researching stress – both occupational and everyday – has spawned a whole host of palliatives, panaceas and placebos designed to enable people to confront stress and to cope. Stress reduction is actually big business – at least, that is, big business in the world of business, if not in the world of education. How stress reduction is attempted, though, varies. At one extreme, one can find the holistic approach to the promotion of personal confidence and positive attitudes routinely characterized as a Japanese approach to occupational adjustment – a mixture of mental menage and compulsory keep-fit programmes. At the other extreme, we can find plenty of evidence of large corporations giving high priority to staff development projects which, based on hard-sell management science, offer job rehearsal, assertiveness training and communication therapy.

In the programme at either end of this continuum, certain taken-for-granted assumptions emerge about how to air or to contain stress. These assumptions tend to centre upon the person, the individual, as opposed to the job or the situation. The emphasis is frequently upon a kind of occupational coaching – upon devising programmes either for extending a person's physical or mental fitness for work or for refining their occupational performance techniques so that they are better equipped to do a good job. We should be cautious here. As we come to introduce the second set of papers in this collection, which all address issues to do with stress reduction in teaching, it is important to keep in mind some of the basic features of the definitions of stress in teaching which have been developed in Part One – the issue of subjectivity and stress, the issue of variation in the levels of stress perception and experience among teachers, and the issue of stress being a product of an interaction between personalities and situations.

If we define stress as a highly subjective experience then we must expect an equally high degree of subjectivity in the ways individuals cope with stress or respond to stress management programmes. As the following chapter by Jack Dunham extensively illustrates, teachers routinely generate a very wide range of strategies for coping with the tensions and pressures of everyday life in school. And what works for one teacher not only might not work for another, but could become an additional source of stress. To be told to 'take a deep breath' as an antidote to feelings of professional isolation or alienation, extends rather than reduces the problematic feelings and perceptions. Nor is such advice appropriate for teachers whose stress level is critical. This is not to diminish the value of relaxation, meditation or other personal strategies teachers use to balance job demands with personal resources. Any extension of the range of resources available to teachers to help them achieve this balance has got to be welcomed and taken seriously. However, we do need to distinguish between intervention strategies aimed at helping teachers cope with what might be called routine stress and those aimed at teachers faced with occupational crises. They are very different, and the skills and techniques which might help teachers cope are cruelly inadequate resources for those who are overwhelmed by stress. Either way, just as in defining stress we asserted a need to be ever vigilant against a temptation to 'blame the victim', so it is with the management of stress. Medical metaphors proliferate in the field and yet, as is also clearly revealed in the following papers, stress reduction in teaching is often a matter of changing the situation rather than of curing the self.

PERSONAL, INTERPERSONAL AND ORGANIZATIONAL RESOURCES FOR COPING WITH STRESS IN TEACHING

Jack Dunham

My research into stress in teaching has revealed considerable differences between teachers in their responses to similar pressures in school; for example, during reorganization and other major changes some teachers reported few signs of adverse reactions and gave several indications of positive responses such as increased zest in their teaching.

These results directed my attention to the strategies teachers use when they encounter heavy work pressures. I found that they were using a wide range of skills, techniques, knowledge, experience, relationships, thoughts and activities, which can be classified as personal, interpersonal and organizational coping resources (Dunham, 1986).

The personal resources are work strategies, positive attitudes and out-of-school activities, including gardening, painting, walking, cooking, baking, cycling, driving their cars fast and praying. The work strategies used in school included clearer planning of what had to be done with specific time allocations and having a clear sense of priorities of what had to be done. Positive attitudes meant, for example:

Recognising the dangers of allowing stress factors to combine in my mind so I reach hyper-self-critical conclusions: I'm under stress → I can't cope → I can't teach → I'm an inadequate person.

The interpersonal resources are social support activities, such as talking over stressful incidents with a friend/husband/wife, meeting people who were not teachers, and using a friend as a 'sounding-board'. Organizational resources came from colleagues in school, from induction and in-service training courses and from advisors and education officers. Support from these sources was apparently considerably less than that obtained from personal and interpersonal resources.

This perspective suggests that coping has two functions. First, coping is concerned with changing a situation which is a source of stress. Secondly, it attempts to deal with the perceptions, thoughts, feelings and psychosomatic reactions which are caused by stress.

Very little research has been conducted which investigates the coping actions used by teachers. Kyriacou (1980) reported a study in which 42 teachers in two comprehensive schools revealed that they used three main groups of strategies: (1) 'Express feelings and seek support', (2) 'Take considered action', e.g. 'Stand back and rationalise the situation', and (3) 'Think of other things.'

The teachers were asked to describe their coping actions and three extracts from their replies provide vivid insights into their attempts to tackle teaching pressures:

1 I talk about outside interests and hobbies and never allow the job to dominate one's life.
2 The working conditions in schools are now a disgrace. The way to survive is to make minimum contact.
3 I usually spend my break with my head on my arms on my desk and wait for peace and tranquillity to take over and renew my strength for my next class . . . my philosophy is that I must survive so I set my sights accordingly and do not attempt the impossible.

My attempts to identify the coping resources which teachers are using to reduce stress are based on two methods. I ask them 'How do you try to reduce your work stress?' and I also invite them to identify their coping strategies on a checklist. Their answers to this question indicate the use of strategies in and out of school in the process of coping with stress, e.g. 72 headteachers of primary schools in two 20-day courses in May 1987 reported the following coping actions:

In school
Making lists of things to do, delegation, task sharing, set up senior management team, talk over problems with colleagues, have priorities and deadlines, say bugger it and go home early, have a laugh, have half an hour off each day, involve governors, complete something worthwhile almost every day.

Out of school
Keep closely in touch with colleagues in area, practise yoga, laugh, drink at home in evenings, consider validity of actions taken in school, draw and paint, do no school work on Saturdays, my family are very good at defusing one, have a night off to go to the pictures/ pub/theatre, gardening, wine making.

The question 'How do you try to reduce your work stress?' was also answered in May 1987 by 70 headteachers of secondary schools, advisors and officers employed by an LEA who participated in a stress management workshop I had been invited to lead. They also were asked to differentiate between their in-school and out-of-school strategies.

In school
Sharing difficulties by talking to colleagues, avoid clutter, denote priority of jobs, delegation, more efficient use of time, write stinging memos to superiors to get things off my chest (I always end up with a positive proposal), accept that industrial action is not personal, timetabling blocks of time for office work, use my switch off (sod it) button, trying to get rules for the game about how priorities are decided (flag documents).

Out of school
Work out of school hours, meditate and pray, relaxation, walking in the country, sharing enjoyment with friends, tranquil home, physical activity, water plants, have an active and interesting life, sleep, massage, sex, yoga, gin, avoid people, try self-hypnosis, creative activities and warn self about stress.

In 1985 I presented a slightly different question to the members of three National Association for Pastoral Care in Education (NAPCE) regional associations who had each invited me to one of their meetings to discuss my work in helping teachers cope with stress. The question was 'How do you cope with the pressures you experience as a result of your involvement in pastoral care in your school?' A total of 52 teachers answered the question. Their replies suggest that some of them had very limited strategies, e.g. 'I try to be more organised.' But other replies suggested a wider range of coping resources. A head of year wrote:

> I keep talking and try to smile. I look for positive signs. I listen to loud music and dig the garden over zealously. I write for new jobs (a change is as good as a rest). I try to organise my teaching day very carefully.

A considerable number of replies relate to in-school coping actions. A head of house enumerated four strategies:

1 Endeavour not to take the member of staff's anger on to myself when dealing with a pupil.
2 To deal in facts.
3 To think positive – that it is only a minority who are causing problems.
4 To try to be consistent.

A smaller number of replies indicate a broad lifestyle approach to tackling work pressures. A deputy head wrote:

1 I get up early and skip for ten minutes, read for fifty minutes; and only then start the day.
2 I relapse into humour; it's fatalism really, but I call it realism – I expect that the worst will happen and then I am pleasantly surprised.
3 I come to sessions like the one you are giving, which not only fuels my humour, but also reminds me that I am in no way isolated (Dunham, 1987).

My second method of enquiry is to ask teachers to identify their coping strategies on a checklist. When I investigated the resources used by teachers in three comprehensive schools, I used the following checklist (Dunham, 1986).

Coping Resources
How do you try to reduce your work stress?
Please tick any of these methods you have used this school year.

1 By learning my job in more detail.
2 By not going to school.
3 Trying to come to terms with each individual situation.
4 Acceptance of the problem.
5 By talking over stressful situation with my husband/wife/family.

 6 By switching off.

 7 Going on a course.

 8 By moving away from the situation completely for a time until the stress has been reduced.

 9 Trying to bring my feelings and opinions into the open.

10 When away from work trying to make sure that I have a good time wherever I go.

11 By involving myself with my family and my own circle of friends when I am not working.

12 Trying to think that I am only human and can make mistakes.

13 Shutting myself in my office.

14 Meeting people who are totally unconnected with teaching.

15 I tend to block out work when I get home and refuse to talk about it.

16 I try to get out as much as possible on the weekend – going for walks, to the museum, to see a film.

17 Forcing myself to take rests before I get tired.

18 By talking about it, usually with colleagues at school.

19 Trying to say 'No' to unnecessary demands.

20 I now admit my limits more easily than when I first became a teacher.

21 At home I try to relax by doing something which gives a simple sense of achievement and success, e.g. baking, knitting, gardening, etc.

22 By setting aside a certain amount of time during the evenings and at weekends when I refuse to do anything connected with school.

23 Any other.

The ten most frequently used coping strategies from this list are shown in Table 6.1.

On the checklist the 'Any other' item was responded to with humour and enthusiasm, and so I was able to compile a list of additional resources:

Meditation; jogging; relaxation; becoming more detached; listen to music; talk to Deputy and Head; live in small community; let off steam verbally; swimming; dance – where great concentration is needed but of a different quality to that of school work; going out and getting drunk; taking the pressure off by playing squash; making love; develop a sense of humour; seek promotion elsewhere; learning greater self-control; writing poetry; grumbling a lot; if I could afford replacements I would probably smash a lot of china.

My two methods of investigation have identified a rich store of resources which teachers use as they strive daily to manage their occupa-

Table 6.1 The ten most frequently used coping strategies.

Coping strategy	Staff usage (%)
1 By setting aside a certain amount of time during the evenings and at weekends when I refuse to do anything connected with school	61
2 Trying to come to terms with each individual situation	52
3 Acceptance of the problem	49
4 By talking over stressful situations with my husband/wife/family	48
5 By involving myself with my family and my own circle of friends when I am not working	47
6 Trying to say 'No' to unnecessary demands	46
7 By switching off	45
8 Trying to bring my feelings and opinions into the open	45
9 I now admit my limits more easily than when I first became a teacher	40
10 By talking about it, usually with colleagues at school	39

tional stress. This information provides a sound basis for anyone wanting to learn to deal with work pressures more effectively. But the demands on teachers appear to be increasing, so it is necessary to seek ways of strengthening coping resources. One way I use is to ask teachers for their recommendations for reducing stress in school.

The NAPCE members were asked 'What recommendations have you for reducing the pressures on teachers involved in pastoral care?' Many constructive proposals were made. The three main recommendations can be summarized as follows:

- more time to do pastoral work so it can be done properly;
- more training; and
- more support.

A head of year recommended:

Much more thought should be given to the proportion of time devoted to teaching/pastoral involvement/preparation generally. All teachers need breathing spaces to cope reasonably with the demands currently made. Much time is spent considering child stress and care (so much is needed) and so little consideration is given to staff health/welfare and esteem. Why should Health Centres run teachers' support groups? They are obviously necessary but surely prove that a weak area exists in the organisation of their schools.

The need for more attention to staff care was also identified in the report of a head of house:

> Support teams should be set up with time to share problems and to define the limits and priorities of pastoral care. This team/group support would reduce tutors' reluctance to discuss what they perceive to be personal failures and would help them to gain confidence and flexibility.

Similar recommendations were made to me by the members of a senior teachers' course in 1987. Their main proposals were:

1 Counselling amongst staff – a sharing of problems.
2 More support offered for staff who are showing reactions to stress.
3 A greater understanding of why stress occurs.
4 Get staff together to talk about any stress they may be experiencing.
5 Sharing fears/problems, etc. with colleagues who are sympathetic to the situation.
6 Improve all teaching staffs' self-esteem.
7 Rationalising work patterns – you can only do so much.

The headteachers of primary schools on OTTO courses I referred to earlier, also put forward guidelines to good practice which would strengthen the personal, interpersonal and organizational resources of themselves and their colleagues. Their major recommendations based on considerable experience were:

1 Do not work in isolation.
2 Have non-contact time for all teachers.
3 Make space each day for quiet reflection.
4 Do not be taken over by the role.
5 Decide not to have a nervous breakdown.
6 Develop interests outside school.
7 Find reasons for pride, satisfaction and confidence.
8 Accept failure and learn from it.

The final recommendations from teachers I would like to discuss are from heads of department. The first is concerned with time management. One head of department argued that 'the control of time is crucial to a teacher's well being' and he asked the question: 'Can teachers be helped towards a more effective and therefore more satisfying use of time?' He proposed the following framework of techniques which he said 'has evolved over fourteen years of teaching'.

1 Be prepared to write down tasks as they are received.
2 Construct a weekly list based on order of importance.
3 Allot tasks to appropriate time slots during the week.
4 Undertake more thought-orientated tasks to times when freshest. If necessary divide up lengthy tasks into small units.
5 Look for tasks that can be discarded or delegated.
6 Identify sources which will enable a rapid and successful completion of a task.
7 Try to avoid taking on more than is reasonably possible to complete.
8 Check off tasks once completed.
9 Try to ensure that some time is left available for emergencies or nothing in particular.

All of the above points relate to a day-to-day, week-to-week basis. Longer-term planning is also necessary. This can be assisted by using a long wall calendar showing completion dates, appointments and special jobs. It may, if displayed in a prominent place within the department, act as an effective form of communicating information to others and so cut out the need for memos.

The second recommendation is concerned with the development of a support group. This head of department wrote:

During the last academic year in the writer's school, a group of teachers, from a wide range of subjects, formed a self-support group. Their aim was to assist each other in the development of classroom skills. Since the classroom is a major source of stressful situations, this seemed a commendable scheme in the fact that it was initiated by themselves and not from senior management. The group members attended each others' lessons as observers and, using a previously drawn up format for classroom teaching, commented instructively on each others' methods and development over the course of the year. Members of the group commented on the following benefits they felt they had received:

(a) identifying skills in others absent in themselves;
(b) becoming aware of pressures faced by teachers in other subjects;
(c) becoming aware of the change in pupils' attitudes with the subject;
(d) being able to offer and accept advice from colleagues in a non-critical atmosphere;
(e) having a feeling that others were interested in your work;
(f) the development of respect, confidence and trust in each others' views and feelings related to their school work.

The positive nature of this group because of all the benefits gained from it can only be fully appreciated by those who took part. It would seem from their comments that many of the benefits not only made them more effective teachers, but gave some degree of release from stress.

These recommendations from heads of department, headteachers, senior teachers, teachers and form tutors provide a valuable bank of resources from which all of us can draw to meet the demands made on us in our work. But it is useful to know that the deposits in the bank can be increased by learning and practising new skills. One of the most important of these will probably be relaxation. Few of the teachers I work with have taken a course in relaxation training. The value of practising to relax is clearly illustrated by brief reports from members of my stress management workshops:

1 Although the influenza bug had lowered my ability to participate fully I found the workshop most helpful. After a very tense rush hour drive back to Nottingham from Sheffield I recalled your relaxation words and was able to continue to an evening committee meeting.

2 I have played your relaxation tape through once and felt quite good. However I do think a great deal of practice is needed. On my return to school on Thursday morning I was immediately inundated with the problems which had built up over the previous two days but was able to tackle them much more calmly. They don't go away, they never do, but I did not end up with the usual splitting headache.

There are several different methods available, some starting at the feet and working upwards and some working from the scalp downwards. There is no 'best' method. Relaxation training involves acquiring skills, e.g. abdomen and chest breathing and 'switching off', that can be used to cope with emotional and bodily reactions in stress situations. It is necessary to practise the relaxation exercises daily until they become effective. The first exercise to learn might be a 'Two Minutes Relaxation Skill':

- Breathe evenly and calmly.
- Think about relaxing your body.
- Think about tension draining from your feet, legs, body, arms, neck and shoulders.
- Notice the tension draining from your body.

The second approach might be that formulated by Murgatroyd and Woolfe (1982):

Relaxation Training Exercises
To practise the routine it is best to lie on the floor or to sit in a position which helps you feel comfortable. Regular practice of this brief routine each day will also aid in the reduction of stress and increase the ability to cope with stressful situations.

1 Lie down on your back or sit in a chair which supports your back.
2 Close your eyes and try to block out any sounds. Think only of these instructions.
3 Think about your head. Feel the muscles in your forehead relaxing. Let any creases just drop away. Relax your eyelids. Relax your jaw. Let your tongue fall to the bottom of your mouth. Begin to breathe deeply.
4 Relax your shoulders – let your arms go loose.
5 Relax your neck – let your head roll until you find a comfortable position.
6 Think about your left arm. Tense it then relax it. Tense it again and relax it slowly. Concentrate on it from the shoulder to the tip of your fingers. Let any tension in the arm flow from your fingers. Let this arm become relaxed.
7 Do the same for your right arm.
8 Think about your left leg from the hip to the knee and from the knee to the tip of your toes. Tense your left leg and then relax it. Tense it harder and then relax it as slowly as you can. Let any tension in this leg flow from your toes. Let this leg become relaxed.
9 Do the same for your right leg.
10 Listen now to any sound from within your body – your breathing, your heartbeat, your stomach. Pick one of the sounds and focus on it. Exclude other thoughts from your mind.
11 After about 2–3 minutes slowly open your eyes, sit upright and stretch your arms and legs fully.

The third type of relaxation training aims at deep relaxation and uses a script I have recorded on tape. I have given tapes to teachers to use at home. The full script for these tapes is available in my book *Stress in Teaching* (1986). It has been adapted from one prepared for management training in industry (Albrecht, 1979).

These three programmes are just a small sample of methods which are available to achieve relaxation. Yoga exercises and meditation are other possibilities. The use of meditation was strongly recommended by a member of one of my primary head courses. He wrote:

> As a founder member of the British Meditation Society I am very interested in informing teachers about the use of meditation as an antidote to and as a preventive measure against stress. I have taught many practising teachers to relax in this way and all find real benefit. The more I meditâte the easier it becomes to cope with stress – I find myself staying calm and controlled in situations where it would be very easy to flare up. Many research projects have shown the depth of relaxation obtained through meditation and doctors are increasingly recommending patients to take meditation.

One meditating skill which this headteacher recommends for learners is sitting on the floor with a straight back and crossed legs, breathing deeply, concentrating on one thought and excluding all others which are trying to intrude. The thought, which is called the mantra, focuses on one word which the learner thinks over and over again for a period of 15–20 minutes.

These relaxation skills might be too passive for some teachers whose feelings of tension, frustration and anger need more active ways of expression. These activities could be directed towards the important aim of becoming physically fit and then maintaining a high level of fitness by physical exercise. Exercise is a potent factor in reducing stress in a number of ways:

1 It strengthens the body against infection by releasing protein from the muscles and preventing the build-up of various steroids including cortisone.
2 It improves respiration by relaxing the diaphragm and activating the lungs which increases the amount of oxygen in the blood.
3 It releases stored up aggression.
4 It restores physical and mental equilibrium.
5 It reduces the risk of stress-associated illnesses and hypertension.

Any exercise which makes you breathe heavily but does not cause you to get out of breath is an effective stress management technique. This means that any activity – jogging, cycling, fast walking, swimming, etc. – can be continued for long enough to bring pleasure and satisfaction without discomfort. There should be at least one of these exercises each day. You might find it enjoyable to begin each day with 'Jack's Six Minute Loosener':

1 *Circular arm swinging*
   • start with arms at side of body,

- swing backwards and over head stretching arms a little as you do,
- arms down to starting position,
- repeat 20 times.

2 *Repeat by going on to toes as arms are stretched overhead*
- repeat 20 times.

3 *Arms by sides*
- allow trunk to fall to left side until fingers touch side of knee,
- resume upright position,
- repeat 10 times.
- *Now use the same exercise to your right side,*
- repeat 10 times.

4 *Arms by sides*
- turn body to left keeping feet still until you are looking immediately behind you,
- return to front position,
- repeat 10 times.
- *Now use the same exercise turning to the right,*
- repeat 10 times.

5 Bend knees keeping them close together with back straight and arms extended forwards – go down as far as you can, come up to a standing position.

6 Gentle running on the same spot until you have counted 200.

These recommendations to learn and to use daily these relaxation and physical exercises are helpful for all teachers who want to reduce stress. But they are of crucial importance to those teachers, heads of department/year/house and headteachers who are workaholics, who might neglect all aspects of their life except work, who are very ambitious, impatient and competitive and who are involved in a 'chronic incessant struggle to achieve more in less and less time' (Friedman and Ulmer, 1985). These so-called Type A colleagues are also coronary prone, i.e. they have an increased risk of all forms of cardiovascular disease leading to heart attacks, compared with Type B colleagues whose lifestyles are the opposite of the overdriven Type A patterns.

These proposals for strengthening personal resources might be perceived as merely palliative and peripheral in their contributions to the reduction of stress in teaching. Teachers who make these comments ask for 'direct-action' recommendations to help them develop school-based strategies and actions.

These approaches to stress reduction are concerned with strengthening organizational resources. This can be achieved by having effective programmes in four areas of staff management – selection, induction, appraisal and training. Each of these is a vital part in an integrated system of staff care and development.

Selection is the starting point of staff development. Mistakes in appointing staff will probably never be eliminated, but the chances of selecting an unsuitable person for a staff management position can be reduced by following a systematic selection process in which each of the stages in the process is recognized to be significant in determining the final decision.

The link between selection and induction is important and if it is weak the advantages of improvements in the selection process may be lost. Strong induction should be regarded as a key organizational resource. Particular attention should be paid to the early identification of gaps in initial training in relation to present job requirements. But induction programmes are also necessary for experienced staff appointed to management roles. For all newcomers an essential part of the induction process is the regular review interview with a senior member of staff. Good opportunities are thereby provided for the satisfaction of important staff needs. These include:

1 Knowing what is expected of them.
2 Receiving feedback about their work.
3 Being able to discuss their difficulties objectively and constructively.
4 Feeling valued by receiving recognition for effort as well as achievement.
5 Being aware of personal and professional growth.

It is a good organizational resource to link the review or appraisal system to in-service training provision so that appropriate opportunities are offered for continuing staff development. For staff appointed to management roles, training in team management skills should be encouraged and the following guidelines are offered as a framework for good practice:

1 Be accessible to staff, do not avoid them.
2 Keep staff informed of pending changes, give them an opportunity to participate in decisions affecting them.
3 Allow grievances to be aired, never ignore them.
4 Give clear instructions that can be understood by all concerned.
5 Discuss the nature, style and quality of work achieved by staff.
6 Encourage new ideas and suggestions and do not be afraid of criticism.
7 Leading a team can be thought of in terms of relationships and trust rather than as mainly a matter of good administration.

These guidelines which emphasize the importance of good relationships in management are supported by research into the characteristics of healthy organizations. In these studies the healthy physical and social conditions in which people should work have been analysed, and they offer clear directions for the development of healthy schools. There are five essential requirements for teachers:

1 They should be able to influence the decisions which affect them at work.
2 In a healthy school they will have a sense of purpose and direction.
3 They should have a strong sense of acceptance and support from their colleagues.
4 Their work enables them to feel competent.
5 They have a rewarding awareness of their own development.

When these requirements become part of the aims of a school for its staff development policies, stress management skills are facilitated because of the encouragement to all members of staff to share information about their pressures and particularly their coping strategies. In a school with these aims, one is less likely to be told by a teacher:

Stress is caused because I am unable to ask for extra support because if I did I would be assessed as a weak teacher by the rest of the staff.

In a school with these aims, pathways of support are opened up in all directions – upwards, sideways and downwards. The sharing of resources between all members of the school community is encouraged – teachers, non-teaching staff and pupils. There is an active policy of participation by all members in the continuing development of the school as a healthy organization.

Each school should establish its own stress reduction programmes. The three aims for these programmes are preparation, prevention and support. It is still true that initial training courses are inadequate in helping their students to begin learning the skills required for effective stress management in teaching. So these gaps in professional training programmes have to be made good in schools. Each stress reduction programme has three phases:

1 *Education*
The first objective is to gain a better understanding of stress. It is not a form of neurosis, not a personality weakness, not an embarrassing state of incompetence. For teachers who associate stress with personal inadequacy or professional failure, acknowledgment of its existence in teaching and acceptance of the need to prepare to cope with it are sometimes strongly resisted. A teacher expressed this perspective very clearly:

Pressure is built into the job. I am well supported but I am also subject to pride which at moments of most need tells me, falsely, that to seek help is to show weakness and that if I can't stand the heat I shouldn't be in the kitchen.

So there is an urgent need to help teachers develop a conceptual framework to understand the interaction between pressures, coping resources and stress reactions. I use an interactionist model as the framework for my initial and in-service training in stress management skills. My definition of stress is that it is a process of behavioural, emotional, mental and physical reactions caused by prolonged, increasing or new pressures which are significantly greater than coping resources. It is important for teachers to learn to identify their pressures at work and to understand their different reactions to these pressures if their strategies are not strong enough. But my main emphasis is on learning new skills, activities and relationships.

2 Rehearsal and application

This phase is concerned with learning and practising new resources which should balance and be complementary to work experiences and they should provide alternative rhythms to the pace of school life. These balancing activities with their alternative rhythms can be found in quite ordinary circumstances which might not be associated with stress reduction – baking bread, polishing a table, scrubbing the kitchen floor and mowing the lawn. They can be found in musical activities, creative work and dramatic performances. They can be developed from relaxation skills and physical exercise.

But it is also helpful in this second phase to help teachers cope more directly with the demands which are experienced in teaching, e.g. dealing with role conflict, change, disruptive pupils, pressures from parents, the LEA and the media, incompetent and poorly motivated colleagues and poor management. Janis (1971) has suggested that this specific preparation, which he called 'emotional inoculation' and the 'work of worrying', should be carried out in three stages:

1 Giving realistic information so that teachers can become aware of the pressures which will be experienced.
2 Giving details of the resources which are available to help them cope with these pressures.
3 Encouraging teachers to reassure themselves by working out specific strategies.

Another strategy which is useful for helping teachers deal effectively with their stressful interactions with colleagues, students, parents and

LEA advisors and officers is known as assertiveness. Being assertive is not the same as being aggressive. Assertiveness has two significant characteristics:

1 Standing up for your own rights in ways which do not violate the rights of others.
2 Expressing your opinions, feelings, needs and beliefs in direct, honest and appropriate ways (Back and Back, 1986).

Typical situations in school in which the quality of assertiveness is valuable in helping to reduce stress are:

(a) When a teacher is blamed for a mistake for which he/she is not responsible.
(b) When a member of staff is asked to undertake a new area of work, despite being over-burdened.
(c) When one is asked to undertake a task within an unrealistic time constraint (Murgatroyd and Wolfe, 1982).

Teachers can also be helped to learn, apply and practise additional coping strategies when schools and LEAs begin to collect materials for in-service training in stress reduction. This process has already started in the Dumfries and Galloway Region of Scotland and the Scottish Health Education Group has produced an in-service training pack on stress which consists of a video and support material. Packages of resource materials for use in staff development work in special schools in the Lothian Region are also being prepared.

Other schools and LEAs wanting to follow these examples of good practice for INSET could include in their packs materials concerned with the following concerns:

What is stress? A check list for identification of pressures in teaching. What coping strategies are used to tackle work pressures? A check list for recognizing the signs of stress if coping strategies are not effective. Recommendations for strengthening coping strategies. The evaluation of these new skills in reducing stress.

The last item is the main concern in the third phase of the development of stress reduction programmes in schools.

3 *Feedback and review*
There are several methods for evaluating the coping skills being used for stress reduction. One way is to compare your performance on the checklists of pressures, coping strategies and stress reactions at the

beginning of the programme with your results at intervals of about a term. Another method is the self-review technique which teachers use after participating in one of my stress management workshops. I would like to use one headteacher's self-appraisal of the benefits of stress management to conclude:

> It helped me personally. Having to draw a graph of my own stress pattern during the last six months made me admit that I have had a pain in the back of my head since December. I have been using strategies of exercise and relaxation but not bothering when I felt too tired. Greater understanding will help me use these strategies more effectively.
>
> I am now also able to recognise that two of our staff are also showing signs of stress – one a probationer and the other a single lady in her early forties. We shall have some meetings which I hope will help them to work out their own strategies.

Conclusions

There is a clear message for me in this self-review and indeed from writing this chapter. Stress can be reduced by strengthening personal, inter-personal and organizational strategies. This can be done by listening to teachers and putting their recommendations into practice. It can also be achieved by learning from other workers in high stress occupations, e.g. nursing, policing and social work. Many potential resources are available to help staff accept present and impending pressures with confidence, competence and effectiveness.

References

Albrecht, K. (1979). *Stress and the Manager*. Prentice Hall: Englewood Cliffs, NJ.

Back, K. and Back, K. (1986). *Assertiveness at Work*. Guild Publishing: London.

Dunham, J. (1986). *Stress in Teaching*. Croom Helm: London.

Dunham, J. (1987). Caring for the pastoral carers. *Pastoral Care in Education* **5** (1 Feb.), 15–21.

Friedman, M. and Ulmer, D. (1985). *Treating Type A Behaviour and Your Heart*. Guild Publishing: London.

Janis, I. (1971). *Stress and Frustration*. Harcourt Brace: San Diego.

Kyriacou, C. (1980). Coping actions and organisational stress among school teachers. *Research Education* **24**, 57–61.

Murgatroyd, S. and Wolfe, R. (1982). *Coping with Crisis*. Open University Press: Milton Keynes.

7 CONTROLLING STRESS

Comment: Now get on with it by yourself.

No area of academic endeavour has been more denigrated in the political debate about education in the 1980s than the social sciences. Sir Keith Joseph took exception to the idea that the 'social' could be studied in any way deserving of the name 'science', while Mrs Thatcher has denied the existence of anything that can be called 'society'. At the very time when politicians are, in a variety of ways, helping to make teaching more stressful, they are also threatening the very academic disciplines which help us to better understand and tackle stress.

In the chapter that follows Hall, Wooster and Woodhouse show that one of the most effective ways of tackling stress is through the application of the insights of social scientists. The method is not, though, to teach students about the 'theory' of stress, but to provide them with learning experiences that encourage them to start putting into practice those personal and social skills that can then be transferred to everyday life so as to reduce and manage stress more effectively.

TAKING RESPONSIBILITY FOR TEACHER STRESS

Eric Hall, Arthur Wooster and David Woodhouse

The deputy head was attracted to the 1-week in-service course by the words 'Counselling Skills' in the title. In her job, she was concerned to improve relationships within her school. She hoped to do this by giving advice, using persuasion and getting her own way. She expected the course to give her the skills to do this. There was an urgent need for change in the school. Morale was very poor, the atmosphere in the staffroom was tense and students were seen as aggressive and unco-operative. The low level of communication and the absence of mutual support among the staff was something she had not met in previous schools.

The apathy of the staff disgusted her. She was desperate to communicate her deep commitment to the staff. When she heard expressions of lack of interest she reacted with fury but, paradoxically, found herself smiling calmly. She raged inwardly at the indifference of colleagues, but held her feelings in check for fear she would erupt and behave aggressively, damaging prospects of communication still further. These were the concerns which propelled her to the course.

The course was one of several, variously titled 'Counselling Skills for Pastoral Care', 'Experiential Approaches to Personal and Social Education' and 'Effective Working Relationships'. These courses shared features in common and consisted entirely of frameworks for experiential learning. In evaluations of their experience of these courses teachers have reported a dramatic reduction in short- and long-term stress.

Stress is almost inevitable. There is now a great deal of evidence to demonstrate that teaching is a stressful profession. Surveys have shown which aspects of teaching are seen as stressful and the psychological and medical problems which result from this stress. This information is reviewed by Kyriacou (1987), but only a small fraction of the research provides the teacher with active solutions. Instead, a picture is presented of the teacher as a passive victim of disruptive students, lack of resources, poor staff communication, industrial dispute and a range of other problems. In this chapter we will discuss ways in which teachers can control stress by taking more responsibility in their lives and increasing the choices they have available to them. We will describe the forms of training that can provide the opportunities for them to learn how to bring this about.

Most of the research findings on stress in teaching are based on responses to questionnaires. This produces a distortion, since, as Smilansky (1984) emphasized, the 'better' teachers reported higher levels of stress. He suggested that the 'better teacher' has the professional confidence to admit to the experience of stress although this may be seen as a weakness by colleagues. We would go further and suggest that teachers need training in the skills of identifying and reporting their experience of stress for a true picture to emerge. When they have these skills they are then in a position to recognize and deal with the reality of the situation, taking more responsibility for their own lives.

Taking control and exercising responsibility

The teacher does not have to be a passive victim of the working situation. People vary in the degree to which they see themselves as being in control of their lives, and from his review of the research Kyriacou (1987) has demonstrated a relationship between a low reported level of stress and the degree to which teachers see themselves as being in control of their lives. Once again this research is based upon questionnaire data involving the problems we have already referred to. In evaluations of our courses, which used extensive interview and diary data, the relationship between reduced stress and assumption of control emerges strongly.

This link between increased exercise of control and reduced stress is built into the design of the course. Structured exercises enable the teachers to become more aware of their own behaviour so that they can see some of the areas in which they create stress for themselves. They can then experiment with alternative ways of behaving and evaluate the outcomes of these changes. It is easier to experiment with new ways of behaving away from the work situation and free from the possibility of damaging relationships with students and colleagues permanently.

Course content

A range of experiential structures was used to provide training in areas such as counselling skills, communication skills, assertiveness training, goal setting, values clarification, non-verbal communication and the use of scripted fantasy. Structures were designed to make the course members more aware of what they were doing, and how self-selected behaviour could be systematically modified. Over and over again members met the opportunity to experience the outcomes of their responses to situations perceived as stressful. One of the main contributions of the training was the direction of the student's awareness to the links between response and outcome. In the light of this awareness it was difficult to avoid the acceptance of responsibility for one's own behaviour.

This emphasis on personal responsibility for learning was achieved by presenting the course members with an open framework to work in pairs or larger groups. The following are two examples of exercises which can be used with a large group on a course.

1 Invite the group to write down a list of the sort of questions they tend to ask of students, colleagues and people close to them. Then form pairs and take turns changing the questions into statements and reading them aloud with the appropriate feelings expressed. For example:

Will you get out your books?
I want you to get out your books.

Can you use your own milk to make coffee?
I don't want you to use my milk to make your coffee.

Are you going past school in the morning?
I need a lift to school in the morning.

2 Invite the group to form pairs. Ask them to fill in a sheet with a series of statements referring to a difficult colleague, a boss, a partner, a friend, a student and a parent, in the form: 'Why you — I feel —' When the list is completed, ask the members of the pairs to take turns at reading the statements, again expressing the appropriate feeling to go with the statement.

These exercises were quoted by course members as being helpful in both the work and home situations. They had contributed to the reduction of stress. With each exercise, the course members could decide for themselves where statements of this nature would be appropriate and helpful. Later, in the small group, newly acquired skills could be tried out as vehicles for the real interactions that were taking place.

The structured exercises were conducted in groups of 30, which meant that the staff member facilitating the session was not privy to, or in a position to interfere with, the learning which was taking place; avoiding leaning over, correcting or supplying answers, or indicating what the learning should be. At the end of a 3-hour session of structured exercises, the group would be brought together and invited to share their experiences. This would bring out the individual differences in learning and no attempt would be made to suggest what conclusions should have been drawn. This is in sharp contrast to the forms of social skills training where the trainer is more didactic and prescriptive. This traditional approach seems to be relatively ineffective in the in-service training of teachers (McIntyre, 1984).

A non-directive method of group facilitation is difficult for some teachers and can arouse negative emotions. The same negative emotions are also aroused in courses that are taught formally, but because of the power structure of the situation are rarely expressed openly. In experiential learning situations the hostility is often expressed directly to the staff and to some extent resolved. This learning about dealing with negative emotions may contribute to the subsequent success in coping with negative emotions in the work setting, which is linked with a reduction in the experience of stress.

Exercises involving drawing, fantasy and touch were included in the structures and often produced a focus on important personal issues. This focus generated a strong emotional component which is not normally an acknowledged part of most in-service courses. These exercises, by avoiding the normal strong use of verbal activity, permit the organization of experience in new forms and old habits are bypassed.

One-third of the course consisted of a small group session. Here the course members were in a much less structured group of between 9 and 13 people with one member of staff. The staff members tended to follow and comment on proceedings rather than initiate them. This was a much more individual experience for the members and, because decisions about the form and content of interaction were left to each person, there was a great deal of confusion.

Group members used the small group in a variety of ways. They compared their self-image with the impressions others formed of them. They used the group as a testing ground for experiments in self-selected change and developed the skills learned in more structured sessions. As this was happening, the staff member attempted to bring the attention of the group to immediate concerns affecting the group as it proceeded (Hall and Hall, 1988).

Evaluating the outcomes

Does this training reduce stress? The main source of evidence regarding the outcomes of training of this nature in relation to the reduction of stress comes from the evaluations of two of these courses which yielded data from 90 teachers. This was obtained using self-report diaries before, during and after the courses (Hall *et al.*, 1984).

Four weeks before the course, individual members were asked to keep a record of their experience in school, particularly noting those events which were personally significant: incidents which might encompass feelings of frustration and anxiety, or incidents left somehow incomplete at the end of a class or a day. These were described under the following headings:

- Incident.
- Action you took.
- Outcome.
- Cause of incident.
- Possible alternative action you might have taken.
- After-effects (stress hangover).

There were spaces for six incidents with students and six incidents with other members of staff. Course members were asked to bring this diary with them on the first day. They were then given a similar diary with the same headings and spaces for six incidents with other members of the course and six incidents with significant people not directly connected with the course. This was handed in on the last day. A third diary was posted to course members 6 weeks after the course. This was in the same form as the first diary.

It was hoped that the diary entries would indicate the attribution of responsibility an individual made concerning each recorded incident. What was clear was that course members had chosen to record incidents which left them in some doubt about their own effectiveness. They tended to indicate a perceived over-reaction when dealing with students and a corresponding under-reaction when dealing with other members of staff.

In the total of 90 pre-course diaries, 327 incidents were recorded. Of these, 187 concerned incidents with students and 140 with other staff members. These reports describe a range of incidents that teachers experience as stressful and show that habitual responses to stressful situations tend to be ineffective, unplanned and potentially damaging to personal relationships (Woodhouse *et al.*, 1985).

Punishment or threat of punishment was involved in 74 per cent of actions taken with pupils as a result of recorded incidents. A total of 33 per cent of interactions with other staff members also involved punishment. While many forms of punishment are available for dealing with students – setting extra work, detention, verbal violence, etc. – the single formal sanction against other members of staff is to report to a senior colleague. Informal punishments are more diverse and include sarcasm, rudeness, 'lecturing' and refusal to cooperate.

The list of incidents which elicit the punishing response and consequent stress reveals a striking similarity between the incidents with students and the incidents with other members of staff (see Table 7.1).

The similarities between these two lists in Table 7.1 is striking, and so are the alternative behaviours which were noted. With students and staff there is the expressed wish to be more direct when confronting conflict. With students this would include a move away from viewing the class as a whole and a move towards dealing with difficulties on a one-to-one basis. With other members of staff, this wish would involve a move away from avoiding conflict – by not dealing with it openly, and then feeling bad about it afterwards – and a move towards the riskier position of making feelings clear to the individual concerned. It is as if both colleagues and students presented course members with a similar set of interpersonal

Table 7.1 Incidents with students and staff.

Incidents with students	Incidents with staff
Disruption of lessons	Disruption of administrative procedure
Aggressive behaviour between students	Aggressive behaviour between staff
Students' refusal to work as directed	'Unprofessional' behaviour of colleagues
Truancy	Covering for absent colleagues

problems. In the case of colleagues, feelings were directed inwards, and in the case of the students, directed to the whole group.

Punishment, in these circumstances, is the automatic response used to reassert control over disruptive or potentially disruptive situations. It is a grossly inefficient tactic. Some success in maintaining the smooth running of the institution may result, but the ensuing stress for the teacher is reported to be high. The legacy of the punishing approach for the person using it was listed as damaged interpersonal relations, alienation, anxiety and personal suffering. These reports make it clear that keeping discipline is that part of the teacher's role which generates the highest levels of stress.

The in-course diaries provided a third list of incidents which are very similar to those listed in Table 7.1:

Incidents on course

Course members disrupting planned structures

Perceived aggression on the part of small group leaders

Arriving late for sessions

Feeling unable to participate

It appears that similar issues are being raised as problematic in relation to students, colleagues and other course members. This would suggest that the course was providing a viable testing ground for work on these issues.

What happened after the course? Thirty-four post-course diaries were returned. Forty-two of the course members were interviewed, many of whom had also returned the diaries, i.e. over 50 per cent of the original number. The interviews took place between 2 and 4 months after the course. Interviewees were asked 10 questions, each of which was followed up by the interviewer with a summary of the content and feeling of the response as he perceived it. This led in some cases to interviews which lasted for more than 90 minutes, depending on the amount of time the interviewee had available and the mutual interest generated in the process of the interview.

In the post-course diaries and the follow-up interviews, reports of stress and notions of punishment disappeared. It is inferred that the course members had made a dramatic shift in their perceptions of their working lives.

Positive changes were reported in 60 per cent of the diaries. They gave specific examples of novel forms of interaction in working relationships as a result of experimenting with new behaviour during the course. The same 60 per cent reported reduced stress and enhanced feelings of well-being as a result of their new behaviour.

A deputy head with responsibility for the welfare of staff and students wrote:

> Since the course there have been dozens of potentially stressful incidents. I have been able to say, 'I think' and 'I choose', rather than 'It's generally known', 'I can't' and other responsibility avoiding statements. This has proved almost 100% successful from the stress point of view. I could not have come through a very demanding period so well but for the six-day course. I would certainly have been more bellicose, curt and domineering.

A teacher who works in a centre for multicultural education notes changes in her behaviour in potentially stressful situations. She reports that she can recognize her own stress reactions and is able to take calm but assertive steps to deal with the situations constructively, with the result that her stress diminishes. She gives the following examples:

> At a meeting of headteachers, a primary adviser and myself, under-currents were being made obvious with regard to channelling me into situations I did not want for personal as well as professional reasons. I felt stressed, but put my point forward coolly and as-sertively rather than aggressively. So far my point of view has been listened to and I have not been 'made' to digress from what I consider necessary work. I realised I was being put into a stressful situation. This realisation helped me to clarify my thoughts and concentrate on the matter in hand rather than concentrating on being stressed. I had valid points to make which I did, and the outcome was that the majority of staff asked me for help with regard to multi-cultural issues. I felt quiet and at ease that I had handled the situation constructively.
>
> Head of section has lots of personal difficulties which make him 'blow his top' over small things. Knowing this, I took more time to make my position clear to him and more time to listen to his responses. This new behaviour has had an effect on the head of section and our relationship, which has until now been poor, has begun to improve. I find him less threatening.

A PE teacher reports the effects of his decision to talk through situations with pupils from whom he would normally expect unquestioning obedi-ence. He noticed that a boy had not taken a shower after a PE session. The teacher would normally have instructed the student to take a shower, but decided to risk a 'softer' approach:

> He showed obvious signs of being upset when I asked him why he wasn't taking a shower. I sat down with him and asked him what had upset him and if he wanted to talk about it. He told me he had a scar from four stitches in his 'bum' and was genuinely upset about people seeing it. I listened and appreciated how he felt and told him so. I did not press him to have a shower, but the following lesson he was one of the first into the shower. Initially I worried how he would feel towards his next PE lesson but the ultimate outcome overcame this stress.

Another very specific outcome:

> One very apparent outcome is my newfound confidence in meetings at school where I am now able to express my point of view without the (at one time) red face and racing pulse.

Some of the reports reflect learning at a more covert level:

> Many of the techniques used on the course I found very powerful in increasing my self-awareness and understanding of other people. The course has led to a re-assessment of myself and a decision to change ways I think and feel which are limiting and constricting me. The experience has increased my self-confidence. I am more willing, and find it easier to admit to feelings of inadequacy or vulnerability – which I find makes me stronger, since I no longer have to use so much of my strength to keep in these emotions.

Of course we have no information about people who were not interviewed and who did not return a post-course diary. However, we are optimistic that many of the non-respondents would also report positive experiences and even those who had difficulties with the course may require time to process their learning. A teacher seconded onto one of our 1-year full-time courses had attended a 6-day course 3 years previously. She told us that her immediate response had been to reject that course as a negative experience but later she found herself making specific changes in her teaching which she directly attributed to insight developed during the course.

A long-term follow-up of the effects of experiential courses for teachers revealed that ex-course members were still making significant changes in their behaviour, which resulted in reductions in stress between 1 and 3 years after the courses took place.

The effects of the small group

All of the course members who were interviewed described the open small group training sessions as the strongest experience and – apart from one person – as a positive learning experience. It was seen as an extremely difficult situation because of the lack of formal guidance about how to behave. All commented on the anxiety generated by being in a position where they were responsible for their own learning. Responses to this anxiety varied: some individuals made deliberate, private contracts to change their behaviour, whereas others, who normally took a passive role, felt that they had to contribute instead.

Several aspects of the small group emerged as sources of positive learning and contributed to subsequent reductions in stress in the professional setting. These include:

1 Directness of feedback, which enabled individuals to check self-perception against the perceptions of others.
2 Absence of restraint in experiments with behaviour due to the relative anonymity of the group.
3 Permission to be aggressive, and the discovery that personal worlds did not fall apart as a result.
4 There were no exercises to hide behind.
5 A reduction of the felt dependence on the approval of authority.

The small group provided the course members with an opportunity to try out skills and changes in behaviour which had been developed in the structured exercises. The lack of structure and the emphasis on personal responsibility seemed to generate a high level of arousal. This emotionality and the direct feedback from other group members provided a strong challenge to habitual ways of behaving and an effective reward for trying out alternatives.

Conclusions

Without exception the in-course diaries report that the course itself was stressful, particularly the small group. However, it provided the course members with an opportunity to work on issues directly related to stress. The stress on the course was short-term and was often dealt with by learning a transferable skill which contributed to a reduction of stress at a later date in the work setting. Ongoing stress at work is often chronic, with no apparent solutions for the removal of the sources of stress.

It is not suggested that all issues can be resolved by experiential learning programmes. Human relationships inevitably involve conflict, which is not resolvable in any final sense. But approaches can be more innovative and can facilitate learning for teachers and students alike. Problems do not have to be resolved in such a way that when one party wins the other loses.

If, as a teacher, you are feeling under stress, it is perfectly all right to have a hot bath, listen to a relaxation tape, go for a run or have a massage. These are passive responses to stress and appropriate when there is nothing you can do to change the source of stress. On the other hand, by changing your contribution to a stressful situation, you may be able to take control of events and reduce stress. Experiential courses provide an environment in which you can increase your chances of doing this.

For the deputy headteacher whose decision to attend the course of in-service training was discussed at the beginning of this chapter, improved discipline, reduced stress and better relationships with colleagues and students did follow (Wooster *et al.*, 1986). This was not by magic, but by improved awareness resulting in responsible choice. She had used goal setting to organize changes in her behaviour. She found colleagues now confided in her and, rather than advising as she had initially planned, she listened and supported their own decision making. She confronted a colleague who was being obstructive and constructively changed the relationships in her personal life.

References

Hall, E. and Hall, C. A. (1988). *Human Relations in Education*. Routledge and Kegan Paul: London.

Hall, E., Woodhouse, D. A. and Wooster, A. D. (1984). An evaluation of in-service courses in human relations. *British Journal of In-Service Education* **11**(1), 55–60.

Kyriacou, C. (1987). Teacher stress and burnout: An international review. *Educational Research* **29**(2), 146–52.

McIntyre, D. (1984). Social skills training for teaching: A cognitive perspective. In Ellis, R. and Whittington, D. (eds), *New Directions in Social Skills Training*. Croom Helm: London.

Smilansky, J. (1984). External and internal correlates of teachers' satisfaction and willingness to report stress. *British Journal of Educational Psychology* **54**, 84–92.

Woodhouse, D. A., Hall, E. and Wooster, A. D. (1985). Taking control of stress in teaching. *British Journal of Educational Psychology* **55**, 119–23.

Wooster, A. D., Hall, E. and Woodhouse, D. A. (1986). In-service courses in human relations: One teacher's learning. *British Journal of Guidance and Counselling* **14**, 1.

8 STRESS AND TRAINING

Comment: This will hurt you more than it hurts me.

In the chapter that follows Esteve advocates tackling stress through Stress Inoculation Training and Systematic Desensitization. Both of these techniques, which have been used for some time in fields other than teaching, share what we regard as the misfortune of the medical metaphor. The danger is that we conjure up images of doctor-like trainers administering suitable treatment either to cure those who experience stress or protect those who might experience it in the future: once the treatment is over all will be well. The pathological view of stress is again encouraged with its attendant tendency to 'blame the victim'.

However, close inspection of the practices Esteve describes here will reveal that both are intended to begin a process which gives the teacher more control as an active agent rather than a passive 'patient'. The sort of training – initial and in-service – Esteve commends is in tune with the action research CRIT advocates: it encourages teachers to inspect and analyse themselves and their classrooms as part of a never-ending cycle of action–evaluation–innovation–action. By such means teachers can win more control over the situations in which they have to work, and both be and feel less victimized.

Ironically, Esteve's call for greater emphasis on the interactional dynamics of teacher–pupil relations in classrooms comes at a time when government policy has been to reduce this element in initial training in favour of 'subject studies'. This shift of emphasis may be a symptom of the long-standing British suspicion of the social sciences which has reached its zenith with the governments of the 1980s. It is not surprising that the initiative and innovations described by Esteve should come from the European mainland where social sciences, and their application to education in particular, have a more secure standing.

Esteve is, for example, Director of an 'Institute of Educational Sciences' – a nomenclature that would probably be regarded as presumptuous in Britain.

TRAINING TEACHERS TO TACKLE STRESS

José Esteve

If we are to tackle the negative effects of teacher burnout we need two kinds of approach. First, we need *preventative* strategies which will have to be developed through initial teacher training. It will be necessary to reconsider some of the aims of such training, to change some of the areas focused on, and to introduce some new areas. If, as I argued in Chapter 1, changes in society have brought inevitable changes to the role of the teacher and to interpersonal relations in education, we must be prepared to rethink initial training for that role in search of more effective responses to the problems of teaching today.

In the second place, it would be worthwhile developing the focus of in-service training to help practising teachers, especially those who so far have not managed to develop a coherent way of dealing with the changes and contradictions in their style of teaching. It would also be for those teachers who, conscious of the lack of means for dealing with situations which arise, are cutting down on what they do and falling into routine patterns as a way of reducing their involvement in problems which are beyond them. Finally, it would help those teachers who live their daily lives dominated by anxiety. Practising teachers also need to assimilate some of the profound changes which have taken place in teaching, both in the classroom and in the society which surrounds them, adapting their style of teaching and the role which they play.

In initial teacher training there are three main lines of action. The first is the establishment of adequate selection procedures for admissions to the teaching profession, based on criteria which rely more on personality than on intellectual qualifications, as is the case at present.

This point, which was mentioned by Wall in a report prepared for UNESCO in 1959, has since become a point of agreement for many researchers, among them Peretti (1982). What is proposed by these authors is that there be established some sort of test based on the personalities of those wishing to become teachers, with the aim of barring those with unstable personalities, and whose fragility would expose them to certain failures within education, as well as possibly multiplying the problems from which they suffer, thus producing negative effects in their students.

As a scientific basis for this proposed initial selection, it would be worth mentioning the work of Amiel-Lebigre (1980) with teachers who received medical treatment for mental disorders, in which it was observed that '60% of a group of 75 neurotic teachers suffered their first psychiatric problems before they began to work in the profession, and that almost all of them (95%) on that occasion consulted a doctor'.

The second proposed line of action is the substitution of a 'normative' form of teacher training by one which is more 'descriptive' in nature. I use 'normative' generically to mean those training programmes which aim towards an 'efficient' or 'good' model of the teacher. This model constitutes a basic 'norm' by which the activities which take place in training are defined, communicating to the future teacher what he/she *should* do, *should* think and *should* avoid in order to approximate what he/she does as closely as possible to the normative model.

This approach is, in itself, conducive to anxiety, in that it implies constant comparison with the model of the ideal teacher, based on the idea that the teacher is the only one responsible for efficient teaching and establishing a direct relationship between the personality of the teacher and the success of his/her teaching.

In a 'descriptive' approach, where success in teaching is seen to depend on the correct action on the part of the teacher, taking into account the conditions which influence the teacher–student relationship as a whole, new teachers who face their first failures will question what they did and look over possible mistakes they may have made in coping with the situation, but they will not begin by calling into question the value of themselves as people.

The third line of action involves making the content of teacher training courses more effective and relevant to the practical realities of teaching. As a starting point, it is proposed that we look at work done on the problems which most affect new teachers, when, after leaving teacher training college or some other institution, they find themselves faced by the real problems of teaching. Honeyford (1982), Vonk (1983) and Veenman (1984) note that there is an emphasis in training on the knowledge of the subject each student is to teach, but that there is a lack of organizational and relationship training. Therefore, students are insufficiently aware of the essential role teachers play in the dynamics of the classroom. They know the subject they have to teach but have little or no idea of how to organize the content of their lessons in order to make them accessible to students of differing levels.

Practical training during the initial period ought to allow the teacher to:

1 Identify him/herself as a teacher and identify the different teaching styles which can be used and the effects these styles produce in the students.
2 Solve problems resulting from the organization of classwork and establish and maintain order in the classroom so that lessons will be as productive as possible.
3 Solve problems resulting from the teaching–learning process, looking in depth at the problems posed by the psychology of teaching and

learning, particularly at the difficulties many new teachers have in organizing their teaching to make it accessible to all of their students.

With respect to concrete techniques which have been employed, both in initial teacher training and in on-going training, to reaffirm the teacher's faith in him/herself and to avoid the accumulation of stress, cognitive techniques have been found to be of great value. Among these, the techniques of 'systematic desensitization' and 'stress inoculation' have already been developed to a certain extent and experience has been gained in their application in teaching training (Esteve and Fracchia, 1986).

As far as avoiding teacher burnout is concerned, in-service teacher training is less important than initial training. Indeed, once new teachers have got over their 'reality shock', albeit by a difficult 'trial and error' approach which is detrimental to themselves, the initial tension is reduced as they begin to feel accepted by students, parents and colleagues alike. Then begins the work of self-realization – exploring a more personal expression of the role played by them in their particular institution.

Good communications between teachers are essential to self-realization. They are the vehicle for self-expression, for sharing problems, and for talking about difficulties and limitations, in order to exchange experiences, ideas and advice with colleagues and others involved in teaching. Poor communications, however, lead to isolation, a common research characteristic of teacher burnout.

Teachers frequently fall victim to routine and boredom, which are real problems when one considers that not only is the social environment constantly changing, but that scientific understanding is continually being updated. To be able to update their teaching in response to a changing environment, teachers need in-service training with its permanent communications network. This should not be limited to academic matters only, but should also include the methodological, social and personal aspects of teaching. Teachers who share their successes and difficulties with each other are able to adapt and improve the aims, methods and content of their teaching. There is much to be gained through this communication, for teachers are able to find out for themselves that pedagogic renovation *does* exist and that it is producing new materials and improving relationships between teachers and students.

Selye (1973, 1976) defines stress as a homeostatic reaction to stimuli of unusual intensity and duration, triggering off a hyperactivity of the homeostatic mechanisms. The feeling of stress passes through three stages: alarm, resistance and exhaustion (the last of which has harmful effects upon the subject). However, Levine (1975) has demonstrated the possibility of adaptation to stress and of developing the resistance of individuals to the point where they are able to cope with stressful situations which previously would have had negative effects upon them.

Polaino (1982) emphasizes the conjunction of stress and anxiety: 'anxiety is the effective and biological consequence of stress, translating into behaviour, but it is at the root of behaviour because it is that that is the cognitive element, intentional and subjective'. The feedback which exists between anxiety and stress is this cognitive element, which differentiates between them. Gaudry and Speilberger (1971), Sinclair *et al.* (1974) and Keavney and Sinclair (1978) emphasize the importance of this cognitive factor, which makes it possible to distinguish between situations which are objectively definable as stress situations, and the subjective perception of such situations, which may make them exaggeratedly menacing or even traumatizing. When the cognitive mechanism is triggered, the subject is liable to threat not so much from the stimuli objectively conceived but from a system which may attribute the quality of personal attack to any given factor. It is thus that the effects of stress can be redoubled, in that the subject may activate alarm responses not only from real threats but also from perceived threats.

It is impossible to anticipate all the potentially conflicting situations which the teacher may face, certainly not in such a way as might enable them to be included in an initial training programme. None the less, research has identified 10–12 specific situations which are liable to become problematic if the teacher is not prepared for them. Certainly, the danger is greater if the teacher reacts by attributing to any such situation the element of threat (Saunders and Watkins, 1980) – hence the importance of cognitive techniques, which reinforce the teacher's sense of security and avoid the accumulation of stress (Coates and Thorensen, 1976; Keavney and Sinclair, 1978; Pagel and Price, 1980; Silvernail, 1980; Morocco, 1982; Friedman and Lehrer, 1983; Côte, 1984).

Coates and Thorensen (1976) analysed the different existing cognitive techniques, and identified the following as being among the most likely to enable young teachers to build up their self-confidence: stress inoculation (Meichenbaum, 1974; Meichenbaum and Cameron, 1977, 1981), an introduction to problem-solving strategies (D'Zurilla and Goldfried, 1971; Goldfried and Davidson, 1976) and systematic desensitization (Goldfried, 1971), coupled with the analysis of classroom interaction and the acquisition of competence by means of simulations. Detailed treatment of their theoretical foundations and their basic utilization can be found in the works of Silver and Wortman (1980) and Capafons and Castillejo (1985).

Stress inoculation training

The process of self-instruction in the inoculation of stress (Meichenbaum and Cameron, 1974) uses a number of techniques for teacher training, such as simulation and role play, in the trial phase which characterizes this method. Training through stress induction is carried out in three stages (Stress Inoculation Training, SIT): modelling phase, learning trial, generalized applications.

Polaino (1982) defines the inoculation of stress as

> a process designed to develop the response capacity of an individual faced by stressful stimuli through a method of behaviour simulation, with the goal of reducing unwanted emotions and of reinforcing an adaptive behaviour.

The process may be summarized as one of developmental presentation of potentially threatening situations to which the teacher must build up a response which can be drawn upon at a later date. The third step in the sequence is extremely important. During this phase, the behaviour of the subject and of others exposed to the same situation is analysed, so as to discover and, subsequently, acquire, resources and procedures which are adequate to the situation. In 1982–3, the Institute of Educational Sciences of the University of Málaga carried out an experiment using SIT techniques, following the guidelines suggested by Harmon-Bowman (1981). In all, the sample consisted of 232 candidates for the Teacher's Certificate. In 1983–4, the experiment was again carried out in a definitive manner with 185 candidates. The following procedure was adopted.

Modelling phase
1 Twelve games with three identical cards were set up, based on the studies of Honeyford (1982) and Vonk (1983). Each game represented a situation regarded as problematic by new teachers and they were graded according to their perceived difficulty.
2 The student teachers were placed in groups of 20–25. The group leader explained the techniques of stress inoculation, and referred to what was known of 'teacher sickness' and the increased levels of stress within the profession. (This explanation drew upon the arguments put forward in Chapter 1.)
3 Emphasis was placed on the competence required to help in stressful situations. This was to be achieved through behaviour analysis carried out by the subject and his/her peer group, so as to reinforce the individual's self-confidence.
4 A general outline for confronting difficult situations in the classroom was then offered, so that teachers did not simply become defensive or act impulsively.

Trial learning
5 This took place outside the seminar room. Identical cards were given to three subjects, in three separate rooms. The cards described a

situation which was potentially one of conflict, and the subjects were given 10, 20 and 30 minutes in which to prepare, in writing, a strategy for dealing with the situation.

6 The other members of the group were not informed as to what was written on the cards. They were asked simply to play the role of pupils of a certain age, and to react as they believed pupils of that age would have done.

7 The three subjects then entered in turn, at 10-minute intervals, the second and third not having seen the previous presentation(s). The three interactions were videotaped to record 'teacher' behaviour as well as pupil reaction. When the first two subjects had finished their presentations, they were allowed to watch their colleague(s).

Generalized applications

8 Each video was played back and all of the participants were asked to note any details which they considered significant to the dynamics of the group, especially the contributions of the 'teacher' and of the 'pupils'.

9 After watching their video being played back to them, each of the three subjects was required to give detailed answers to the following questions (in the order in which they made their presentations):

  (a) How do you see yourself in your presentation? (*Objective*: to allow the future teacher to identify his/her pedagogic style.)

  (b) What was the main idea behind your presentation? (*Objective*: to prepare the future teacher for analysis of as many significant factors as possible in a given situation, reinforcing the idea that the control of situations may stem from the number of prior analyses constructed.)

  (c) Did the pupils respond as you expected or did you have to modify your thinking in the course of your presentation? (*Objective*: to draw attention to the dynamics of the classroom and the capacity of all elements to contribute to that dynamic.)

  (d) What skills or resources did you find the most useful in this situation? (*Objective*: to analyse how the mastery of situations of conflict may depend on the use of adequate or inadequate resources, according to context and to the totality of elements in play.)

  (e) In the light of what you saw of your colleagues' performances, what resources did they draw upon which might have been used usefully in your situation? (*Objective*: to reinforce the previous objective and to make the point that competence can be acquired, e.g. from observation of the behaviour of others and from the analysis of the reactions which they evoked, as well as introducing any given strategy at the right moment.)

10 The entire group was invited to respond to questions (d) and (e) so as to reinforce generalizations. It is extremely important to warn all participants that they are not sitting in judgement on a colleague's performance, but that they are to carry out an objective analysis of the resources which appear to be more or less useful in the situations in which the three subjects were placed. The group leader has to be prepared to intervene forcefully on this point if necessary during stages 9 and 10. There has to be a constant emphasis on resources and skills, not performance; this is supportive of objective 9 (e).

If any one of the subjects expresses strong dissatisfaction with his/her own performance, he/she should be encouraged to try again. This provides an excellent opportunity for observing what has been learned from experience (both the student's own and from observation of the experience of others).

Evaluation of the SIT programme by the 1983–4 cohort provided the following responses:

1 On the interest of the topic (multiple-choice response):
  very interested: 137 (74.05 per cent)
  moderately interested: 47 (25.40 per cent)
  not interested: 1 (0.54 per cent)
2 To the open question, what had most interested them during the theory part of their course, the SIT was ranked:
  in positive terms: 163 (88.11 per cent)
  in negative terms: 5 (2.70 per cent)
3 Did they feel that the SIT programme was relevant to teaching?
  yes: 172 (92.97 per cent)
  no: 3 (1.62 per cent)
  no reply: 10 (5.40 per cent)
4 In an open question about desirable changes in the theory component of their course:
  more time should be given to SIT because of its relevance to teaching: 107 (57.83 per cent)
5 In the final part of the evaluation, calling for free comment under the heading 'observations':
  83 students (44 per cent) emphasized the practical value of SIT in reinforcing their self-confidence in respect of the first years of teaching. It should be added, that this idea had been stressed a number of times during the modelling phase by the group leader, as indicated under objective 9(c). For this reason, no specific question on the issue had been included, so as not to bias the results.

It is clear that an evaluation of this sort allows us to do no more than claim the apparent acceptance of the programme by those who experienced it. An examination of the extent to which learning was internalized would require the adaptation and use, under test and post-test conditions similar to those of Harmon-Bowman (1981), of the Self-Control Schedule of Rosenbaum or of techniques of evaluating stress in teachers developed by Pettegrew and Wolf (1982).

The Institute of Educational Sciences of the University of Málaga is presently carrying out a new evaluation of the SIT programme, following those teachers trained with this technique during their first year in teaching. Three methods are being used:

1 A comprehensive questionnaire about his/her situation in the school and in the classroom, including items about relationships with pupils, colleagues and principals.
2 Diaries of the personal and professional experiences of the new teachers during their first year of teaching.
3 An analysis of the content of tapes recorded during the development of discussion groups, in which five new teachers meet once a week for 45 minutes to talk about their experiences in the school during the last week.

In this way we hope to make a valid comparison of teachers trained with the SIT programme with other new teachers trained with an over-idealistic pre-service training.

When failure in teaching persists the dominant feeling the teacher experiences is that of helplessness. A real fear of teaching develops and, finally, several affective, motivational and behavioural problems appear: there is a decrease in motivation, effort and job satisfaction.

The teacher's way of understanding this state of affairs leads to a subjective perception of teaching situations which makes them exaggeratedly menacing or even traumatizing. Subjectively perceived threats may, then, be as important as 'real' ones in activating alarm responses which escalate the effects of stress in the burnt-out teacher.

Teachers in this situation characteristically develop the cognitive mechanism of approximation-avoidance, wherein a full recognition of the problem is repressed and instead a partial, more bearable picture is substituted. It has been shown in the proposed model for understanding teacher stress that those most likely to experience burnout are teachers with a positive attitude to teaching, and who are concerned to remain committed to teaching and to realize their ideals, but who, at the same time, are not adequately prepared to cope with difficult situations. Consequently, such teachers continually experience failure. If they do not employ evasive strategies, like inhibition or routine, the mechanism of approximation-avoidance is finally developed. The teacher wants to help pupils but at the same time is confronted daily by failure: the result is anxiety.

Systematic Desensitization

1 *First Interview*
The first step in systematic desensitization is to identify the specific situations which are liable to become problematic if the teacher reacts by attributing to the situation a subjective element of threat. Each teacher must be interviewed in order to determine his/her specific fears and those situations to which he/she attributes a major traumatic significance.

2 *Discussion groups*
In practice we cannot expect that complete information will be obtained from the first interview, even if the interviewer is working with a good questionnaire and asking the burnt-out teacher about those factors which, frequently, pose difficulties during teaching.

The idealistic conceptions of teaching accepted by teachers often inhibit them from speaking about their failures and recognizing that they have difficulties in certain situations which they are not able to bring under control. For these reasons we utilize discussion groups, which have two functions: (i) to provide more complete knowledge of the specific aspects which each teacher deems traumatic or threatening; and (ii) to begin desensitization in the presentation of teaching problems, breaking the habit of isolation and putting the teacher in touch with others who have had similar problems.

The work in discussion groups has two objectives:

- Self-monitoring of teachers, in which the subjects observe and register the behaviour requiring modification.
- Self-evaluation, in which the teacher learns to find his/her own objectives for the modification of behaviour.

From these objectives the subject can evaluate if he/she is changing their behaviour in the classroom successfully.

Discussion groups consist of four or five burnt-out teachers, who meet once a week and record their teaching problems. Usually, three sessions of 90 minutes each are adequate, though an additional session may be employed if necessary to accommodate every teacher's contribution. The interviewer does not normally take part in the discussions, but only participates in the proposal of new subjects for discussion, or in the case of serious trouble during discussions.

Only with discussion groups can we reach a full understanding of the situations which create problems for each teacher and their relative importance. Each discussion group session starts and finishes with relaxation exercises using the techniques developed by Wolpe (1982, 1984).

3 Hierarchy of anxious situations

After the discussion groups are completed, each teacher takes part in a second personal interview. The objective of this interview is to help teachers in the elaboration of a hierarchical list of those situations with which they have problems of anxiety.

Each teacher's subjective perception of each situation is rated using 5-point intervals from 0 to 100 so that a score of 5 represents a situation deemed more easy and 100 represents the most anxiety-provoking situation.

4 Training in muscular relaxation

We use the method described by Wolpe (1982), based on the previous works of Jacobson, but with the advantage of condensing the method into six sessions. All teachers are requested to practise the exercises at home, twice a day for 15 minutes, following the shortened form of relaxation instructions recorded on tape.

5 Practice in imagination

After training in muscular relaxation and before applying systematic desensitization, teachers are trained to develop their ability to evoke scenes in their imagination as graphically as possible, erasing them later and replacing them by others. It is very important to use only neutral or pleasant scenes, never situations which produce anxiety.

6 Systematic desensitization in imagination

(a) The session starts with the usual shortened form of relaxation instructions, followed by the muscular relaxation exercises.
(b) After relaxation, the teacher is requested to imagine the least anxiety-provoking situation on his/her subjective scale for 5–7 seconds. After this time, the teacher is then requested to erase it and to concentrate all of his/her attention on muscular relaxation and, having achieved relaxation, to sustain it for 1 minute.
(c) The second item on his/her subjective scale of anxiety is not taken until he/she is able to imagine the first scene, twice consecutively, without experiencing anxiety. On the second occasion, the teacher must imagine the scene for 10–15 seconds.
(d) If, at any time, the teacher shows anxiety, the entire process is

immediately stopped, and he/she is asked to concentrate on his/her relaxation exercises until deep relaxation is achieved.

(e) If anxiety appears in the first presentation of an item, this must be attempted again after a condition of deep relaxation has been achieved.

(f) If anxiety turns up again in the second evocation of the same item, a state of relaxation is induced and we return to the last preceding item on the subjective scale of anxiety.

(g) In each session only three or four new items must be performed.

(h) All sessions must finish with a positive experience. If the last item performed evokes anxiety, a state of relaxation is induced and we ask the teacher to imagine the last preceding item.

(i) At the end of sessions, the shortened instructions are again followed by the relaxation exercises.

(j) The next session begins by repeating the last item in which desensitization was achieved in the preceding session (Wolpe, 1982).

7 Systematic desensitization in practice

If, over a period of time, a teacher experiences accumulated anxiety, it should not be expected that they can, after a process of desensitization, experience a problem-free return to teaching. Experiments in France (Mandra, 1984) suggest the need for a period of retraining, in which the teacher is not required to take complete responsibility for a class and, helped by others, faces up to real situations before they can produce disarming anxiety. Relaxation exercises must be used frequently during this period. It is considered necessary to continue this retraining period for 6–12 months.

Neither of the two techniques, stress inoculation training or systematic desensitization, has magical properties, but they may be invaluable elements in our approach to stress, by providing teachers with the resources, time and encouragement to analyse their own practices and develop their skills accordingly.

Teacher burnout, however, will not disappear until society increases its support for and recognition of the work teachers do. The key to teacher burnout lies in the devaluation of teaching as a profession, and in the poor working conditions teachers face in the classroom, which oblige them to perform in a mediocre way, for which, then, paradoxically, we hold them responsible.

References

Amiel-Lebigre, F. (1980). Psicopatologia de la función docente. In Debesse, M. and Mialaret, G. (eds), *La función docente*. Oikos-Tau: Barcelona.

Capafons, A. and Castillejo, J. L. (eds) (1985). *Autocontrol y Educación*. Nau Llibres: Valencia.

Coates, T. J. and Thorensen, C. E. (1976). Teacher anxiety: A review with recommendations. *Review of Educational Research* 46, 159–84.

Côte, R. L. (1984). Changements observés chez des enseignants(es) participant à un programme d'éducation émotionnelle RADIX. Actes du 3ième congres de l'Association International de Recherche sur la Personne de L'Enseignant, Université de Mons.

Esteve, J. M. and Fracchia, A. F. B. (1986). Inoculation against stress: A technique for beginning teachers. *European Journal of Teacher Education* 9(3).

Friedman, G. H. and Lehrer, B. (1983). The effectiveness of self-directed and lecture/discussion stress management approaches and the locus of control of teacher. *American Education Research Journal* 20, 563–80.

Gaudry, E. and Speilberger, C. D. (1971). *Anxiety and Educational Achievement.* John Wiley: Sydney.

Goldfried, M. R. (1971). Systematic desensitisation as training in self-control. *Journal of Consulting and Clinical Psychology* 37, 228–34.

Goldfried, M. R. and Davidson, G. C. (1976). *Clinical Behaviour Therapy.* Holt, Rinehart and Winston: New York.

Harmon-Bowman, M. (1981). *Stress Inoculation Training: The Effect of Self-efficacy and Education Treatment on Trainee Performance.* Indiana University: Indianapolis.

Honeyford, R. (1982). *Starting Teaching.* Croom Helm: London.

Keavney, G. and Sinclair, K. E. (1978). Teacher concerns and teacher anxiety: A neglected topic of classroom research. *Review of Educational Research* 48, 273–90.

Levine, S. (1975). Psychosocial factors in growth and development. In Levi, L. (ed.) *Society, Stress and Disease Vol. 2*, New York: Oxford University Press.

Mandra, R. (1984). Causas de inadaptacion y desadaptacion de los enseñantes franceses y dispositivo de ayuda puesto en marcha por el Ministerio de Educacion Nacional. In Esteve, J. M. (ed.), *Profesores en Conflicto.* Narcea: Madrid.

Meichenbaum, D. (1977). *Cognitive Behaviour Modification: An Integrative Approach.* Plenum Press: New York.

Meichenbaum, D. (1981). Una perspectiva cognitivo-comportamental del proceso de socialisación. *Análisis y modificación de conducta*, No. extra, pp. 85–105.

Meichenbaum, D. and Cameron, R. (1974). The clinical potential of modifying what clients say to themselves. In Mahoney, M. J. and Thorensen, C. E. (eds), *Self-control: Power to the Person*, pp. 263–90. Brooks-Cole: Monterey.

Moracco, J. C. (1982). The counselor's role in reducing teacher stress. *Personnel and Guidance Journal* 60, 549–52.

Pagel, S. and Price, J. (1980). Strategies to alleviate teacher stress. *The Pointer* 24(2), 45–53.

Peretti, A. (1982). *La Formation des Personnels de L'Éducation Nationale.* La Documentation Française: Paris.

Pettegrew, L. S. and Wolf, G. E. (1982). Validating measures of teacher stress. *American Educational Research Journal* 19, 373–96.

Polaino, A. (1982). El estrés de los profesores: Estrategias psicológicas dede intervención para su manejo control. *Revista Española de Pedagogia* 40(157), 17–45.

Saunders, R. and Watkins, J. F. (1980). Teacher burnout/stress management research: Implications for teacher preparation, personnel selection and staff development. Paper presented at the National Conference of the National Council of States on Inservice Education (ED. 225940).

Selye, H. (1973). The evolution of stress concept. *Scientific American* **61**, 692–9.

Selye, H. (1976). *The Stress of Life*. McGraw-Hill: New York.

Silver, R. L. and Wortman, C. B. (1980). Coping with undesirable life events. In Garber, J. and Seligman, M. E. P. (eds), *Human Helplessness*. Academic Press: London and San Diego.

Silvernail, D. L. (1980). Assessing the effectiveness of preservice field: Experiences in reducing teacher anxiety and concern levels. Paper presented at the Annual Conference of the New England Educational Research (ED. 191828), Lenox, MA.

Sinclair, K. E., Heys, T. A. and Kemmis, S. (1974). Anxiety and cognitive processes in problem solving. *Australian Journal of Education* **3**, 239–59.

Veenman, S. (1984). Perceived problems of the beginning teacher. *Review of Educational Research* **54**, 143–78.

Vonk, J. H. C. (1983). Problems of the beginning teacher. *European Journal of Teacher Education* **6**, 133–50.

Wall, W. D. (1959). *Education et Santé Mental*. UNESCO: Paris.

Wolpe, J. (1982). *The Practice of Behavior Therapy*, 3rd edition. Pergamon Press: New York.

Wolpe, J. (1984). Deconditioning and *ad hoc* uses of relaxation: An overview. *Journal of Behavior Therapy and Experimental Psychiatry* **15**(4), 299–304.

D'Zurilla, T. J. and Goldfried, M. R. (1971). Problem solving and behaviour modification. *Journal of Abnormal Psychology* **78**, 107–126.

9 STRESS AND EDUCATIONAL CHANGE

*Comment: The task ahead will not be done, nor well done without the
initiatives, efforts and commitment of the education
profession, in particular teachers in the classroom*
(DES, 1987, The National Curriculum 5–16).

*In the editorial commentaries we have made in this book, we have tried to identify
certain themes in relation to the study of teaching and stress which we think are
highly significant and which link the separate contributions to this collection.
Some issues have received particular emphasis: that stress is subjective; that it is a
consequence of an interaction between the individual and the situation; that
though endemic in teaching, stress can be managed and reduced. We have also
noted that stress in teaching is a dynamic condition, related to changes and
readjustments in education and that, in this sense, it has a decidedly political
reference. Certainly, teachers themselves demonstrate an awareness of how stress
in teaching is politically charged; many of the accounts and stories they produce
to express how they feel about their work centre on precise references to the
policies and projects of those who control education. In the final chapter, which
is a kind of postscript to the book as a whole and was written after the conference
on which the volume is based, Martin Cole sets out to chart the main political
changes he sees as developing outside the education system in Britain but which,
nevertheless, have direct implications for how stress is manifest in teaching
in the foreseeable future and for how teachers cope with it. Stress is subjective,
but we might need to move beyond the personal if we are to control its incidence
and impact.*

Reference

Department of Education and Science (1987). *The National Curriculum 5–16.*
HMSO: London.

THE POLITICS OF STRESS IN TEACHING

Martin Cole

'Prevention or cure? Which are we looking for?' The question was posed more than once at the conference which gave birth to this book. Usually it referred to a debate about the most effective 'solutions' to stress, but I want to argue in this chapter that the question encapsulates a dilemma of much larger dimensions. 'Stress', I hope to show, is a political issue.

To say that the way we choose to react to a psychological phenomenon like stress is a political matter is not to say anything new but it is to remind ourselves of something easily and often overlooked as it was, in my view, at the conference. This was a critical flaw at a time of radical political and social change when education is high on the political agenda. Indeed, I shall argue later that a major and often unrecognized source of teacher stress in the 1980s has been the political battle being fought over the values that should be enshrined in our education system.

Stress becomes a political issue from the moment we define it. This happens because our definition must address the question of the relationship between the individual and society, i.e. the relationship which is at the heart of the essential and everlasting political dilemma. Our definition of stress in turn leads towards particular locations of the 'problem' of stress: essentially the question is whether we locate the problem in the individuals or in their environment. From our location of the problem follows our view of suitable treatment. Finally, our treatment becomes political in its influence on the relative power individuals and society can bring to bear on each other.

If, when teachers find a situation stressful, we look to the pathology of the individual for an explanation and remedy we leave the situation (classroom, school and education system) intact: the status quo is preserved. Individual teachers, we assume, must adapt themselves to the situation. But an analysis that locates the cause and the solution in the essentially stressful nature of the situation in which teachers are obliged to operate provides the potential for change: situations, we now assume, must be adapted to the emotional needs of individuals.

A great deal of rapid change is, of course, occurring currently in the world of education. There is little evidence, though, to suggest that the needs of teachers under stress have been a prime concern of the change-makers. Indeed, it has been argued elsewhere in this volume (see chapters by Cox *et al.*, Kyriacou and Woods) that change in education has become a major new source of stress for teachers in the 1980s.

We must draw the important distinction here between the *process* of change itself and the new conditions and new stability that might ultimately ensue when change is complete. After all, if the effect of all the educational change of the 1980s was to produce a new stability in the 1990s in which teaching was a less stressful occupation than before, teachers might come to feel that all the traumas of the 1980s had been worthwhile in the long-term. But *is* that the likely future? What will be the effects of present changes on teachers' work – to make it more, or less, stressful?

In order to answer these questions in the space available we need an overview of the many and massive changes in the 1980s. Two key concepts provide this overview: centralization and privatization. At first the two concepts may appear contradictory: centralization leading to greater state control, but privatization to more client (i.e. parent) control. I shall argue, though, that in practice these twin policies of the Conservative governments of the 1980s interlock and support each other.

Centralization refers to the reassertion of government control over expenditure levels, curriculum, examinations, school management and teachers (the latter through control of training, appraisal and career structure). The imposition of standardized testing backs up these controls. Privatization includes the Assisted Places Scheme, City Technology Colleges, the delegation of financial control to schools, alongside reduced central funding, and the proposal that schools be able to 'opt out' of LEA control.

The twin policies interlock because the effect of free-market competition between schools, to impress parents and attract pupils with good test and examination results, will be to encourage schools to become more like the institutions government wishes to see. Centralized power has been used to effect the growth of privatization; a privatized education system it is believed will help to deliver the curriculum, assessment, teaching methods, etc., which government favours but knows its centralized power alone cannot produce.

Proposals for more open enrolment in schools seem to be located just at the point where the twin policies of centralization and privatization interlock – parents' power to choose schools for their children will, government believes, ensure that schools are judged by and, therefore, adhere to, the national curriculum and its associated testing and examinations. Although the government's rhetoric stresses parental choice and power, a scrutiny of legislation leaves one in little doubt that the proposed function for the great majority of parents (i.e. those in the state sector) will be to act merely as 'watchdogs' monitoring schools' delivery of centrally determined curricula; there appears to be little scope for parents to have an innovative role.

We may conclude this brief overview by noting that these twin policies in education are entirely consistent with the broad thrust of government policy: a more liberal approach to the economy and a more authoritarian approach to social control.

How will this double-barrelled attempt to change British education affect teachers' experience of stress? At first there appear to be grounds for thinking that, once complete, some of the changes currently under way, or likely to be implemented shortly, will reduce stress in teaching. They would do this by reducing the number and intensity of some of the 'endemic uncertainties' of teaching, as Lortie (1975) calls them. Among these uncertainties which are inherent in teaching are the 'intangible goals' given to teachers. Thus what children should learn, and how, is controversial, ambiguous and multi-faceted, since it may include social, moral, emotional and aesthetic dimensions. This kind of uncertainty leads to corresponding doubt as to how teachers' worth can be measured, by themselves or others. Not only are the goals often intangible, and their achievement therefore difficult to measure, but the timing of educational assessment is problematic: the real fruits of a teacher's work with a pupil may not be apparent until years later. All of this contributes to the role-ambiguity which, it has been argued (for example, by Capel and Woods in this volume), is an important source of stress in teaching.

The effect of a more clearly defined national curriculum, accompanied by standardized testing at 7, 11, 14 and 16 could be to reduce some of these uncertainties about teachers' goals and the extent to which they achieve them. Indeed, many teacher-training students (whose inexperience makes the endemic uncertainties even more daunting) have told me that they welcome the national curriculum and some of its attendant testing because 'at least we'll know where we stand: what's expected of us, and exactly how we're going to be judged as teachers'. For successful teachers, at least, the future would appear less stressful as they come to receive more precise positive feedback that boosts self-esteem.

However, this possible reduction in role ambiguity is counterbalanced by a potential increase in role *conflict*, another well-researched source of stress for teachers, in which there is disagreement with (and perhaps between) colleagues over what one should be doing and how. Centrally controlled, standardized curriculum and testing, supported by teacher appraisal, reduce the scope for the exercise of teachers' individual autonomy. The particular form of the role conflict which is exacerbated in these circumstances is that between the 'system' or institution and the individual's own ideal identity of him/herself as a teacher.

To complete the picture of future levels of stress in teaching we must turn to one of the other 'endemic uncertainties' Lortie defines. Particularly relevant here is the unclear demarcation of the teacher's responsibility for the quality of the 'end products', the pupils and their learning. Teaching is only one part of the process by which the child is socialized, some would argue one of the less important parts. Parents, peers, neighbourhoods, the mass media, and society at large are all involved in the process, sometimes more powerfully than the teacher. Children, moreover, mature of their *own* accord. This makes it difficult for the teacher to judge his or her contribution to the child's development and also leads to a *lack of control* over the process.

Here is the crux of the matter. As several contributors to this book (Kyriacou, Freeman, Capel and Cox *et al.*) show, an important source of stress for teachers is the feeling that they are not in control of the situation in which they have to operate. Teachers have always had a relatively low degree of control over the child's development, but the effect of government policy in the 1980s is to reduce that control still further. Central control of curriculum and examinations, reinforced by parental power at the local level, will reduce teachers' control over exactly what they teach their pupils, how and when. Teachers' skills (and the pride taken in them) of adapting the curriculum and teaching methods to the particular needs of individuals and groups, and testing them appropriately, will be undermined.

The future of teaching, then, seems to represent the worst of all worlds. Teachers are to be *more accountable* and their work assessed more rigorously, and exposed more publicly, but they are to have *less control* over the means of producing the results by which they will be judged. The combination of greater demands and a sense of diminishing power to match up to them promises to make teaching even more stressful in the future.

My view that teaching is likely to become increasingly stressful is not based simply on the 'mechanics' of the way education is controlled, for the mechanics are but manifestations of the *meaning* given to education by policy-makers and their supporters. It has not always been appropriate to talk about the meaning of British education policy, since for much of the present century government policy on education has been piecemeal and pragmatic. There may from time to time have been controversies over particular reforms (comprehensivization, for example) but we have not previously seen the present situation – sweeping, radical, rapid and comprehensive change, and change not simply in the machinery of state education but also in its fundamental aims. It has now become appropriate, therefore, to talk of a government ideology of education, for that is what the panoply of interwoven contemporary changes constituting centralization and privatization represents.

The crucial point for those of us concerned with the stressful nature of teaching is that this 'new right' government ideology of education is at odds with the ideology of the teaching profession. Of course, to talk of an ideology of the teaching profession is to commit a rather crude generalization. Teaching attracts people with widely divergent political sympathies but, nevertheless, there do seem to be some values and attitudes concerning education that unite British teachers generally, however much they might disagree about other areas of policy. These values and attitudes can be detected in the way teachers talk about themselves and each other: about their motives, their satisfactions and dissatisfactions. They are expressed also by applicants to teacher-training institutions when interviewed about their reasons for wishing to become teachers. The ideology is also implicit in much of the academic and professional literature produced for and by educators. Certain key ideas, phrases and words constantly reappear.

Perhaps the central idea in this ideology of the teaching profession is the belief that education should be a liberating experience for the child – freeing the child from the limitations of existing knowledge, experience or aspirations. The key phrases that express the idea are 'widening horizons' or 'raising the sights' of the child, 'independence of mind' or 'the capacity to think for oneself'. The focus here is very much on the individual and a belief in the individual's right to the opportunity to develop personal potential, talents, interests and aspirations as far as possible. For most teachers this belief entails the principle of equal opportunity for all children regardless of the accident of birth that assigns them to a particular social class, gender, religious or ethnic group. Many teachers reveal a particular concern for extending equal opportunity to disadvantaged children such as those from homes unsympathetic to education or those with learning difficulties.

If this is the dominant ideology of British teachers it must also be said that many of them experience frustration and disillusionment at the persistent way in which pupils' academic attainment continues to correlate very closely with social class and ethnic origin and, to a lesser extent, with gender. One of the reasons suggested for this continued inequality of achievement is that the curriculum and examination system puts manual workers' children, children of ethnic minorities and girls at a disadvantage. Many believe that the present centralization of control over curriculum and examinations, and the standardization that will result, will only make these matters worse.

Some of the best evidence of the ideology of British teachers in action has been seen not in formal teaching situations but in the extracurricular life of schools. The tradition of vocational obligation among teachers lays great emphasis on activities such as attending to pupils' mental, physical and social welfare by the establishment of close and caring relationships beyond those of a purely pedagogical nature. Teachers often see themselves as surrogate parents or social workers providing therapy for troubled children; they care about what happens outside the classroom. Playtimes and school meal-times are seen as opportunities to practise this wider professional function. Many teachers give up some of their own time to put on plays and concerts, supervise inter-school sports matches, take children on educational visits at home and abroad, organize camping expeditions, arrange fund-raising events, join parents in social functions, etc. These voluntary activities are a most important element in the ways teachers assess themselves and each other. It is also the means by which they maintain, individually and collectively, an image of themselves as dedicated, altruistic professionals. Teachers use the phrase 'nine-to-four teacher' to refer disparagingly to a colleague who, by leaving school as soon as lessons are over and not taking on the additional tasks listed, fails to show the breadth of commitment they expect. There is perhaps a symbolic significance in the way teachers have withdrawn from these voluntary activities during the industrial action of the mid-1980s: it is *their* way of trying to prove their true worth. Significantly, this withdrawal appeared to cut little ice with government.

In many long, confidential interviews conducted with teachers it has become very clear to me that for many teachers job satisfaction rests heavily on pride taken in the attempt to practise this liberating, child-centred and altruistic ideology. Only when that sort of intrinsic reward is in short supply do questions of the level of extrinsic reward like pay become predominant.

The crisis for British teachers today is that both their intrinsic *and* extrinsic rewards are under attack. The decline in the extrinsic reward of pay is annoying in itself, and in that it is seen as evidence that teachers' professional worth is not recognized. Declining recognition and respect attacks the teacher's own identity and the sense of his or her own personal worth – an important element of intrinsic reward. Worst of all, perhaps, teachers see the ideology of their profession, again a source of identity and the sense of personal worth, under concerted attack by government. While teachers aim to liberate children, government appears more concerned to restrain them; where teachers focus on individuals' needs, potential and aspirations, government seems concerned only to subordinate children's development to provision for society's needs (or, rather, a partisan view of society's needs); where teachers are concerned with promoting the development of the whole person, government seems interested only in ways the person can be made more exploitable economically. The government's immovability in the face of the mid-1980s industrial action suggested it placed little value on teachers' voluntary and pastoral activities: only the basics of pedagogy mattered. Finally, and perhaps most woundingly of all, the government's privatization policy seems dedicated to efficiency and uncaring of equality of opportunity.

Perhaps the best way of describing the effect of this ideological rift between government and teachers is to allow a teacher (or rather, by now, *ex*-teacher) to explain for himself. In this extract from a letter written to *The Guardian* in the midst of the industrial dispute in 1985, a senior teacher shows that his decision to leave the profession is due more to the loss of intrinsic rewards than the loss of extrinsic ones:

Because I'm fortunate enough to be on top of Scale 4 I even earn enough to get by. Since I achieved my promotion early I think it reasonable to assume that I might be successful if I chose to press for a deputy headship and even a headship. So why am I leaving teaching?

The rewards in teaching have always been a complex mixture of pay and job satisfaction. Recently for me both have declined. I've always gained a lot of my job satisfaction through the things I've done with school children after school hours: school teams, drama, clubs, societies and trips. Over the last five years these have been increasingly disrupted. Of course I could ignore union action and go on with things – at least those that don't involve anyone else – but to do so would imply my satisfaction with current attitudes to education and pay levels, so instead I cut off my nose to spite my face. Besides which, Sir Keith Joseph and his fellows really do not care what kind of an institution a school is, a caring community or an education factory. Provided teachers are willing to grind into pupils what HM Government thinks is important, HM Government will be content, and the more cheaply it can be done, the more content it will be.

I never expected teaching to be easy, and I suppose that however hard it might have become it would never have been as hard as my first year when I was put under such personal strain that survival was all I cared about. I was prepared to put up with that, prepared to throw myself with my colleagues into all sorts of extra-curricular activities, prepared to wade through mountains of exercise books and piles of preparation because we had a vision of a school as a caring, developing community and we enjoyed being part of it.

I'm not prepared, though, to put up with the shabby books, even shabbier classrooms, and dilapidated furniture to serve the new educational vision known as 'spending cuts'. I'm not prepared to be the object of insult and innuendo from my employers who think they can starve us all into a new contract that doesn't involve a fraction of the professionalism we were willing to give.

I am sure that this teacher speaks for very many of his colleagues, but represents only the most drastic response to the ideological rift: the decision to leave the profession. For most of today's teachers, at a time of high unemployment and qualified for few other occupations, leaving the profession is not a realistic option. The future for those who stay in the profession looks like one of still greater stress and still lower morale as the difficulties inherent in teaching become still more difficult to bear. Note that the author of the letter referred to 'personal strain' and 'survival' in a job he 'never expected . . . to be easy', but that he was 'prepared to put up with that . . . because we had a vision of a school as a caring, developing community'. Many teachers have shown in interviews with me that it is their 'vision' of what they are doing as a teacher that sustains them when their work is stressful. After a bad day in the classroom when, perhaps, the children have been difficult to control or the quality of their work disappointing, teachers find consolation in the belief that theirs is in the long run important work, that they are providing a valuable service for their pupils, and that they have society's respect for what they do.

Such beliefs have been undermined by recent developments so that many teachers now find it difficult to believe in their profession or themselves. We must remember, when observing that role conflict is an important source of stress in teaching, that one very important set of expectations that may be involved in the conflict is that of the individual teacher himself or herself. For many teachers, for whom teaching was an ambition they grew up with from an early age, their personal identity is inseparable from their professional identity so that when the latter is threatened so, too, is the former. The teacher's crisis of identity can, then, have far-reaching repercussions, spilling over from one's professional life into one's personal life.

The prospects for a bridging of the ideological rift I have described in the foreseeable future do not seem good. Those who imagine a change of government would immediately heal the breach, should note that the opposition parties in the 1980s have not challenged the principles of centralization policy, only the details (though they have attacked the fundamentals of privatization). It should also be remembered that many aspects of centralization policy were advocated by the 1970s Labour government of James Callaghan, whose Ruskin College speech in 1976, heralding the 'Great Debate' on education, might be considered a key moment in the opening of the rift between the government and the teaching profession.

Of course, another way in which the ideological rift could be closed would be if the ideology of the teaching profession came to resemble more closely that of government. Could this happen if, for example, teaching began to attract a new kind of entrant characterized by the values of authoritarianism and competitiveness rather than the liberalism and egalitarianism I have suggested typify the profession at present? I find it difficult to imagine what would motivate this new breed to become teachers. Ironically, in view of the stance 1980s governments have taken to teachers' pay, one of the few factors that might attract this new breed of teacher would be a high salary and status – if they existed!

Any change in the ideology of the teaching profession, however achieved, would be a long time coming. For the foreseeable future the burning issue will be the increasing levels of stress experienced by teachers and our response to that problem. I hope that the above remarks have established that the issue is much more than one of simply finding an effective 'treatment' for teachers under stress. Indeed, those who offer teachers courses devoted simply to relaxation techniques, hints on diet and exercise, and advice on the therapeutic use of leisure time, could be unwittingly *adding* to the conditions that generate stress in the first place. Their failure to address the *situation* which is stressful, or to see it as part of the 'problem', effectively supports the stressful status quo or represents an acquiescence in the changes being imposed on teachers' work which promise to make that work still more stressful. All of us, then, who seek to explain stress in teaching and offer 'solutions' must recognize the political implications of our thoughts and actions.

The political nature of our reactions to stress are but one manifestation of that fundamental dilemma which is at the heart of the political choices that face every state, every social organization, every family even. It is the dilemma about the rights of the state, to collectively impose itself on the individual, as opposed to the individual's rights of freedom of thought, word and deed – that divides capitalism and socialism, totalitarianism and democracy. The dilemma is ever-present in every society but its particular contemporary significance for us is that at a particular moment in history a particular government, taking a rather different approach to this dilemma from that of most teachers, has exposed the dilemma more clearly at the junction of the state and education system and given it more direct, practical importance for teachers.

But we must remember that just as the dilemma is ever-present in society so is it ever-present in the microcosm of the school and of each classroom. When the teacher is faced with pupils who do not want to behave as society thinks they ought, or when they do not want to learn what society thinks they ought to learn, it is the fundamental dilemma of the relation between the state and the individual that the teacher is being asked to manage in the small world of the classroom. Teachers are right at the heart of the confrontation between the collective and the individual. Their position is essentially conflictual. They are torn between the children and the state in their sometimes incompatible desires. Surely few occupations place their workers in such a fundamentally conflictual position? It is this situation which makes teaching an inherently and inevitably stressful occupation.

Although I argue (with Woods in this volume) that teaching will always be stressful, I have also tried to show that at particular historical times certain circumstances may critically add to the stress teachers experience. One of those circumstances is that pertaining in Britain today, when there is a dissolution of the consensus between government and the teaching profession about the general approach to be taken to the political dilemma they both at their different levels face. This analysis implies, of course, some ways in which levels of stress currently experienced by teachers could be reduced. Hence my assertion that any attempt to understand or treat the mental health of teachers must take account of the broad social and political context in which teachers operate, and must recognize that teachers' work is dominated by the fundamental political dilemma that confronts every society and all of its constituent institutions.

We need, I believe, to talk not so much of a pathology of distressed teachers as of a pathology of distressed education systems and of distressed societies.

References

Lortie, D. (1975). *Schoolteacher: A Sociological Study*. Methuen: London.
The Guardian (1985). Letter from Owen Temple, July.

INDEX

Japanese approach, 117
job description, 44, 57
job performance, 29, 44, 57–8, 70
job rehearsal, 117
job satisfaction, 29, 57–60, 63, 66, 78,
    105–6, 166, 167
Johansson, G., 100
Joseph, Sir Keith, 135, 167

Kahn, R., 37
Kallen, D., 17
Keavney, G., 150
Klugman, E., 18
knowledge, 9, 13–14
Knutton, S., 30, 32
Kremer, L., 31, 100
Kyriacou, C., 27–32 passim, 37, 41, 61, 77,
    84, 91, 99–100, 106, 110, 119, 136

labelling (of teachers), 3, 92
Labour government, 168
Lacey, C., 87
Lader, M. H., 77
Laslett, R., 31, 106
Laughlin, A., 30, 31, 100
laughter (coping mechanism), 83
Lawrenson, G., 37
learning
    experiential, 136–45 passim
    trial (stress inoculation), 151–2
leisure facilities, 109, 110, 124
Léon, F., 15
Levine, S., 149
Lidermann, E., 77
life events, 76–7, 78
local education authorities, 44, 45, 74
Lock, L., 88, 89
locus of control, 37–8, 40–4, 46, 60,
    63–5
Lortie, D. C., 50, 163

Mace-Kradjian, G., 15
McIntyre, T. C., 28, 100, 138
Mackay, C. J., 101
McKinnon, A., 37
McNamara, 92
Mahoney, P., 88
'man-job fitness', 78
management
    organizational strategies, 100, 107–10
    role, 32, 90
    science, 117
Mancini, V., 39
Mandra, R., 157
marital status, 72–3, 76
Martens, R., 37
Martinez, A., 14
Maslach, C., 30, 41
Maslach Burnout Inventory, 30, 41

mass media, ix–xii, 9, 14
Maxwell and Cox Associates, 109
measures of stress, 29–30, 41
media, ix–xii, 9, 14
meditation, 127–8
Meichenbaum, D., 150
mental health, 19, 21, 35
    behavioural patterns, 77–8
    goals, 80–1
    stress-reduction approaches, 78–80
    study data, 68–77
Merazzi, Claude, 8, 10
middle-class values, 9–10
MISPE/60 questionnaire, 15
Mitter, Wolfgang, 6
modelling phase (stress inoculation), 151,
    153
Moracco, J., 31, 150
morale, 6, 31, 89, 96, 135, 167
    boosting (coping strategy), 52
Morris, P., 53
motivation
    pupil, 13, 30–1
    teacher, 32, 58
Murgatroyd, S., 127, 133
Murphy, E., 77
Mycroft, A., 30, 32

Nagy, S., 37–8
National Association for Pastoral Care in
    Education, 120, 123
national curriculum, 160, 162, 163
National Curriculum, The (DES), 160
National Education Association, 17
National Health Service, 69
negotiation (coping strategy), 52, 89
nervous breakdown, 69, 71, 77, 80
New Society, x
New Teacher in School, The (DES), 91
noise levels, 58
non-survival, survival and, 92–4
non-teachers (sources of stress), 105
normative mode, coping as, 52–3
normative training, 148

occupational health, 107, 108
occupational therapy, 52, 93
OECD report, 6
organizational
    psychology, 107
    strategies, 100, 107–10
    variables (environment), 38, 39–40,
    46
Osler, W., 77
OTTO courses, 124
out-of-school strategies, 120, 121, 123
overload, 39–40
Owen, W., 29
Ozga, J., 91

INDEX 175

Pagel, S., 150
parental choice/power, 162, 164
Parkes, C. M., 77
participative approach (problem-solving), 101
pastoral care, 32, 120, 123–4
Payne, R. L., 27, 28, 31, 32, 58, 61, 100, 110
Peretti, A., 147
performance, 29, 44, 57–8, 70
    see also competence
Perrins, Richard, 89, 90
'personal enrichment', 95
personal qualities, 91–2, 96, 147
personal resources, 84–5, 118–29 passim
personality, 49, 76, 78
    type A, 38, 77, 129
    type B, 77, 129
Pettegrew, L., 61
physical exercise, 44, 128–9
physical factor (burnout), 38
physical illness, 69, 72, 73, 74, 76–7
Pines, A., 38, 39
Plowden Committee, 86
Polaino, A., 150, 151
politics of stress, 160–70
Pollard, A., 52, 86
Pont, H., 32, 100
Porter, J. F., 8, 16
post-course diaries, 141–3
Pratt, J., 29, 30, 77, 99, 100
'praxis shock', 15
pre-course diaries, 139–40
preventative strategies, 147
Price, J., 150
primary factors (burnout), 7, 16–18
primary school, 86
primary sector, 100
priorities, 51, 61
private medical services, 108
privatization, 162, 164, 166, 168
problem-solving, 53, 54, 56, 57
    approach, 99–111
promotion, 74, 79–80
psychological domain (self-help), 109
psychological factor (burnout), 38
psychometric testing, 78–9
punishment (stress incidents), 140–1
    see also discipline
pupil
    discipline, 17, 31, 86–7, 88–9, 140–1
    management, 26
    motivation, 13, 30–1
    removal (coping strategy), 52
    responses (to authority), 86–7, 88–9

qualifications (teacher), 12, 13
Quinn, R. M., 77

race factor, 10, 87–8

Rahe, R. H., 76
Ranjard, Patrice, 11, 13
reality, idealism and, 49, 50–1, 60–5
'reality shock', 14–15, 149
recipes for action, 51
recreation facilities, 109, 110, 124
redefinition of situation, 92
rehearsal phase (stress-reduction), 132–3
Reid, G., 32, 100
relaxation training, 44, 54, 126–8, 156–7
researching stress, 35
    causal factors, 36–46
    idealism challenged, 48–67
    mental health, 68–81
resignation, 29, 69, 74, 76
resistance (stess stage), 149
resocialization, 49, 62, 66
resources, 16
    allocation, 51, 92
    for special educational needs, 62, 64
retirement, early, 29, 69, 74, 76, 91
retraining period, 157
retreatism, 92
review interview, 130
review phase (stress-reduction), 133–4
rituals, 49–51, 52, 59–60, 67
Rizzo, J., 41
role ambiguity, 36–7, 38, 40–4, 46, 163
role conflict, 32, 36–8, 40–4, 46, 64, 84–5, 163, 168
    production of, 86–9, 95, 96
role factors, 61, 64
role play, 46, 151
Role Questionnaire, 41
Rosenbaum, 154
Rosenman, R. H., 77
Rosser, E., 89
Rotter, J. B., 37, 41
Rotter Internal-External Locus of Control Scale, 41
routine, 19, 21, 52
Roy, W., 91

salaries, 12–13, 31, 91, 166–7
Saunders, R., 150
Savicki, V., 38
'school fitness', 80
schools
    culture of, 10, 11, 49, 50
    'healthy', 130–1
    holidays, 22, 29
Schwab, R. L., 37, 38, 40, 46
Scottish Health Education Group, 133
secondary factors (burnout), 7–15
secondary schools, 36–46
Secondary Schools Advisor, 102, 103
secondary sector, 100, 105
selection process, 78–9, 80, 129–30, 147–8
Self-Control Schedule, 154